We Are the Church:
A History of the Diocese of
OAKLAND

BY JEFFREY M. BURNS AND MARY CARMEN BATIZA

Front cover photo :
Bishop Floyd L. Begin arrives via helicopter in 1962
in the new Oakland Diocese to be its first bishop.
(John Wright photo)

Publisher	Éditions du Signe – B.P. 94
	67038 Strasbourg – France
Publishing Director	Christian Riehl
Director of Publication	Dr. Claude-Bernard Costecalde
Publishing Assistant	Audrey Harrer
Design and Layout	Sylvie Reiss
Copyright Text	© The Diocese of Oakland, 2001
Copyright Design and Layout	© 2001 Éditions du Signe
ISBN	2-7468-0627-4
Printed	in Italy by Arti Grafiche

TABLE OF CONTENTS

Celebration of the Centennial of the City of Oakland at St. Francis de Sales Church, 1952

PREFACE

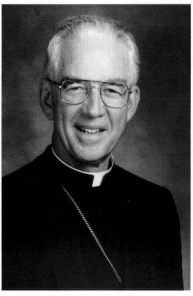

Dear Remembering People or diocesan celebrants:

*M*emory is a great human faculty and equally treasured gift. Ordered and arranged, it becomes history.

With this present volume we acknowledge our indebtedness to Jeffrey Burns who has sifted the experiences of forty years. As archivist of the Archdiocese of San Francisco, he has reached into the early Catholic presence at Mission San Jose in 1797 and St. Mary's Oakland, 1853. He has, however, the long view of the religious story of Alameda and Contra Costa Counties which far back belonged to the ecclesiastical province of Sonora, Mexico. With the help of our Oakland archivist, Mary Carmen Batiza, Doctor Burns has fashioned both the picture and the context of our diocesan years.

"Memory performs the impossible for us," stated the American critic Van Doren, "holding together past and present, giving continuity and dignity to human life." Macauley, the great British historian in the nineteenth century, previewed that assessment fearing that his history of England might be seen as "having descended below the dignity of history."

Cervantes, three hundred years earlier, added what for us is a particularly pertinent dimension, that, "history is a

sacred thing." He meant "insofar as it contains truth." His sentiments, however, indeed agree with our own intuition that the story of a diocese is also the discerning of the actions of God's ever present grace.

Sacredness is one perception. We recall also the observation of Samuel Johnson, "The recollection of the past is only useful by way of provision for the future." Pope John Paul II reaffirmed the observation, "To remember the past is to commit oneself to the future."

We pay tribute and thanks to those who have written this history from the time of John XXIII in January of 1962 and the arrival of our first bishop, Floyd L. Begin from Cleveland in April of the same year. May the memory and accomplishments of all in the diocese inspire us for the years ahead and stir our hopes and gracious response to the call of mission in our own time. To many, as well as to our historians, we appreciatively say thanks for the memory.

Sincerely,

John S. Cummins
Bishop of Oakland

CHAPTER 1

INTRODUCTION

The Diocese of Oakland was born on the eve of the Second Vatican Council in an era when the Church in the United States was prospering mightily.

All quantitative indicators suggested a flourishing church—Mass attendance was high, Catholic societies and devotions were thriving, vocations to the priesthood and sisterhood were plentiful, and it seemed that new Catholic schools and churches were being dedicated each month. For Catholics in the Bay Area, as for Catholics throughout the United States, the future seemed bright with promise. As journalist John Deedy put it, "Ours was a rose garden and it was in full bloom until the mid-1960s. It was a great time to be Catholic in the United States." The opening of the Second Vatican Council seemed to promise greater and greater things. Few realized that the Council would fundamentally change the direction of the Church. The Church in the Diocese of Oakland in 2002 was to be quite different from the Church that existed when it was founded in 1962.

For some, the changes initiated by the Council proved difficult, but the new Diocese of Oakland accepted the changes with optimism and enthusiasm. Since its inception, what has

Mission San Jose: where it all began

distinguished the Diocese of Oakland has been its openness to, and its implementation of, the decrees of the Vatican Council. In its scant four-decade history, the diocese has earned the reputation of being a "Vatican II Diocese." This achievement is due in no small measure to the leadership of its two bishops—Floyd L. Begin (1962-1977) and his successor, John S. Cummins (1977—). Both Bishops became known for their openness to new ideas and their respect for the opinions of their clergy and laity. The Vatican II concept of "shared responsibility" was very much at home in Oakland. As Bishop Cummins reflected in 1992, "Bishop Begin was open to new initiatives, and he gave freedom to try new things, a quality widely appreciated, indeed cherished and guarded carefully to the present." As such, consultation and innovation have always been part of the Oakland Catholic experience.

But the history of the People of God in Alameda and Contra Costa Counties did not begin in 1962; their history extends back to 1797 when the first Catholic foundation was made at Mission San Jose.

Bishop Begin with the future Bishop John Cummins

The Pilgrim Image of Our Lady of Guadalupe passes beneath the Bay Bridge during Jubilee 2000 celebration (Arturo Vera photo)

Cardinal Eugenio Pacelli blesses the Bay Bridge, 1936: San Francisco Archbishop John Mitty (to Pacelli's right) and New York Cardinal Francis Spellman (left) look on

MISSION SAN JOSE

Lasuen wrote, "I blessed the water, the grounds, and a large cross which we venerated and erected, in a beautiful place called *Oroysom* by the natives, some of whom were present and showed themselves well pleased... Immediately afterwards we sang the Litany of All Saints, and celebrated the holy sacrifice of the Mass in an *enramada* which we set up the preceding evening and decorated it from floor to roof with many different flowers." Soldiers from the San Francisco presidio, and about seventy Christian Indians, brought from the neighboring Mission Santa Clara, attended.

On June 11, 1797, the feast of the Holy Trinity, Franciscan Father Fermin Francisco de Lasuen, the successor of Father Junipero Serra as father president of the California missions, established Mission San Jose, the fifteenth of the California missions, in honor of "our glorious patriarch St. Joseph."

San Carlos Borromeo, which served as Serra's headquarters. The Spanish spent the next several years exploring the region surrounding the San Francisco Bay—in March 1772, the expedition of Pedro Fages and Father Juan Crespi celebrated the first Masses in what later became the Diocese of Oakland. In 1776, Mission San Francisco de Asis was established, with Mission Santa Clara established the following year. It was not until twenty years later, however, that Mission San Jose was established.

The establishment of Mission San Jose was part of the Spanish imperial plan to settle and occupy Alta California (the present state of California). Although the Spanish conquest of Mexico had begun in 1519, the Spanish had demonstrated little interest in settling their northernmost territory until 1769, when Father Junipero Serra, accompanied by Captain Gaspar de Portola, established the first Spanish settlement in Alta California at San Diego. The following year, a presidio at Monterey was established as well as a mission at Carmel named

The mission was the central institution in the Spanish plan of settlement. Its main goal was to convert and pacify the native peoples, which involved a dual process. First, the missionaries had to evangelize and convert the native peoples to Catholicism and to nurture their new found faith. Second, they had to teach the neophytes (newly converted Indians) European ways, particularly the industrial and agricultural arts. The Spanish believed that for conversion to take root, a cultural as well as religious conversion had to take place. A new way of life had to accompany the new religion. The arrival of the Spanish fundamentally altered the native way of life, shattering their world and world view.

The Native Peoples

The native peoples that inhabited the Bay Area were called "Costanoan" (the coast people) by the Spanish, though they called themselves the Ohlone. They lived in small groups or tribelets consisting of about 100 to 400 people. The Bay Area consisted of many different tribelets speaking distinct and different dialects. The local tribelets were hunters and gatherers who lived off the abundance of naturally occurring foodstuffs. Women gathered seeds, nuts, berries, roots, and acorns, while men hunted for elk, deer, bear, antelope and fished in the local streams, lagoons, and bay. The dependence on nature created an intimacy and knowledge of, and respect for, the natural world that was reflected in their religious and ecological systems. In the native world, nature was alive with spirits.

The Spanish regarded the Indians as a primitive and simple people and had little respect for their culture or their religious beliefs.

Mission Life

Two young padres were sent to staff Mission San Jose, Fathers Isidoro Barcenilla and Augustin Merino. They received an initial endowment from Missions San Francisco and Santa Clara of cattle, sheep, horses, mules, grain and corn. By September they baptized their first convert, a Native American woman named Gilpae, reported as being twenty-four years old, and "from the Redwoods." She was given the name Josefa by Father Magin Catala, "the holy man from Santa Clara," who had come from the neighboring mission to perform the first baptism. By the end of the year, thirty-two additional native peoples had converted. By 1802, 406 neophytes were present at Mission San Jose.

Native dancers at Mission San Jose 1806
(Courtesy of the Bancroft Library)

Father Narciso Duran extends a gift to a Native American child (Photo courtesy of the Huntington Library)

Joining a mission meant adopting a whole new way of life, a life which included a regimented work schedule, instruction in farming and in industry, punishments for not adhering to mission rules, a different diet, and restrictions: once baptized, one was not allowed to leave the mission without the permission of the padres. If one left, he or she would be sought out, returned to the mission, and punished.

Indians who made the decision to convert became part of the mission routine, which consisted of work and prayer. In addition to daily prayer, Indians tilled the fields, worked in the shops, tended the livestock, or worked at

workshops, barracks, etc.. Most important, they constructed the mission church. The Mission San Jose church took four years to complete and was dedicated by mission president Father Esteban Tapis on April 22, 1809.

Despite the initial success in gaining converts, mission life proved difficult for the young padres. Barcenilla and Merino lasted less than five years each, due to poor health brought on by the strain of establishing the mission. Several other padres served until Fathers Buenaventura Fortuny and Narciso Duran arrived in 1806. These two padres provided remarkable stability with Fortuny remaining until 1826 and Duran until 1833.

Mission San Jose circa 1855

constructing the mission buildings. A Russian visitor in 1806 recorded, "The works to which the [neophytes] are principally employed are husbandry, tending the cattle, and shearing the sheep, or in mechanical trades, as building, preparing tallow and soap, or making household utensils…The most laborious employment, which is grinding the corn, is left almost entirely to the women…." Besides providing the workforce for the missions farming and industries, the neophytes built all the mission buildings: rectory,

Under their guidance, Mission San Jose grew to be one of the largest and most productive missions in California. By 1810, the mission contained 545 neophytes and was producing more than 4,000 bushels of wheat a year. By the mid-1820s Father Duran boasted that the mission was producing 10,000 to 15,000 bushels a year of wheat, corn, grain and barley. By 1831, the mission hosted a neophyte community of close to 1,900, while the mission herds contained more than 12,000 cattle, 13,000 sheep, and 13,000 horses.

While the mission community prospered materially, it suffered a depressingly high death rate. The neophyte community was devastated by a variety of European diseases including measles, influenza, tuberculosis, dysentery, cholera, and venereal disease. In 1806, a measles epidemic wiped out one-fourth of the neophytes. Between 1800 and 1810, while 1,745 natives were baptized, 1,192 died. From 1806 to 1831, 6,637 were baptized, but the mission population increased by only 1,224. Father Duran lamented in 1814, "I am weary of so many sick and dying Indians, who are more fragile than glass." By 1820, the Ohlone people had been reduced to less than one-fifth of their pre-mission

and figured music; as also in the playing of almost any instrument." Duran boasted, "The feasts of the Church are celebrated with a decency and a majesty superior to anything which the land seemed to promise." Visitors to the mission praised the choir, one noting that they "performed very well indeed," and another that the music was "well-executed."

One of the more troubling aspects of mission life was the relationship between the missions and the military. Though military presence at the missions was limited, military dominance in the area was necessary if the mission agenda was to advance. At the time of the establishment of

Mission San Jose Interior

population. To maintain the mission population, the padres recruited other, more distant tribes including the Patwin, the Yokuts and the Miwoks.

On a more positive note, Mission San Jose, under the direction of Father Duran, developed the most impressive music program of any mission. Duran wrote liturgical music specially suited for the neophytes, and created an orchestra which included fifteen violins, three violoncellos, flutes and drums. He noted, "...the singers and musicians are trained from boyhood with considerable ease in both plain

Mission San Jose, one of the local tribelets threatened to kill any tribesmen assisting in the construction of the new mission. A visit by the Spanish army suppressed this opposition, and mission development continued. Mission San Jose's location at the gateway to the San Joaquin Valley made it the staging ground for Spanish forays against the interior tribes who were accused of raiding Spanish lands and stealing Spanish horses. Expeditions were conducted against the interior tribes in 1813, 1816, 1819, 1823, and 1826.

In 1829, one of the largest Native American rebellions took place at Mission San Jose under the leadership of a neophyte named Estanislao. Estanislao gathered a large army of runaways from Mission San Jose, Mission Santa Clara, and Mission San Juan Bautista. Two Spanish expeditions failed to subdue the rebels until a young Mariano Vallejo brutally suppressed the rebellion with the third expedition. Interestingly, Father Duran called for an investigation of Vallejo's activities, accusing him of committing several atrocities and demanding that Vallejo be punished. He was not. In addition, the notorious rebel leader, Estanislao, returned to the mission, where he was received by Duran, who obtained a pardon for Estanislao. Estanislao lived at the mission until his death from small pox in 1839. According to one historian, "Duran was one of the most vigilant of the missionaries in defending Indian interests."

Be that as it may, the missions would be closed by 1836. In 1821, Mexico had achieved its independence from Spain, and factions began to work to "secularize the missions," that is to close and dismantle the mission system. Secularization meant removing the temporal power of the missions and reducing them to the status of ordinary parishes; Indians were to be released from the missions, free to go wherever they desired. In theory, the Indians were to receive allotments of land and livestock from the mission holdings, as mission padres believed the land and livestock belonged to the neophytes—they had just been holding it "in trust" for them until they were ready to use it. In practice, the neophytes received little benefit from secularization. "Hispanic elite families" seized most of the land and cattle.

The condition of the California Indians worsened with the closing of the missions.

In 1833, the Mexican government decreed that all the California missions were to be secularized. By 1836, Mission San Jose was closed, though the chapel remained open with a resident priest in attendance. The Mexican administrators appointed to oversee the secularization process did little to assist the neophytes. A British naval officer observed in 1837, "Lately, all the missions have been transferred into the hands of administrators, who, under the new law, take about two-thirds to themselves, and account for the remaining third to government. The consequence is, that the Indians are robbed…" And in 1841 an American military officer observed, "The administrators have made themselves and those by whom they were appointed, rich upon the spoils of these missions; and so great have been the drafts upon some of these missions, that they have not been able to support the neophytes. The mission of San Jose, for instance…was obliged to order off five hundred of its proselytes to procure their subsistence as they best could." According to Randall Milliken, many of the neophytes drifted back into the Central Valley, while others found work as menials on the new ranchos. By and large, the secularization of the missions did the native peoples no favor.

Mission Church rebuilt 1985

The closing of the missions necessitated the creation of new church structures for the state. In 1840, the first California diocese, the Diocese of *Ambas* (both) Californias, which included all of Baja and Alta California, was formed. Veteran of the California missions, Father Francisco Garcia Diego y Moreno was named the first bishop of the vast diocese, and set up his headquarters at Santa Barbara. Garcia Diego y Moreno suffered through a very difficult episcopate before dying of tuberculosis in 1846. The diocese was left in the hands of his able assistant, Father Jose Gonzalez Rubio, OFM, who served as administrator until 1850.

The mission continued to have a resident priest until 1845; then it was ministered to by a priest from Mission Santa Clara. The same year, the mission lands and buildings were sold by the Mexican governor for $12,000, but the sale was nullified the following year and the land returned to the church by U.S. Army General Stephen Kearney, who arrived during the war with Mexico. In 1846, war had broken out between the United States and Mexico. Northern California fell to United States forces with practically no resistance. Sonoma, Sutter's Fort (Sacramento), San Francisco, and Monterey quickly came under U.S. control.

The war ended in 1848, the same year that gold was discovered. By 1849, the mission buildings were being used as a place of lodging for gold seekers and for a general store. By 1853, the mission became St. Joseph's parish in the newly created Archdiocese of San Francisco. In 1858, the Archbishop of San Francisco, Joseph Alemany, succeeded in getting the Federal government to validate the church's claim to the twenty-eight plus acres of Mission San Jose.

The chapel that had been constructed in 1809, continued to be used as the parish church until 1868, when it was destroyed by a terrible earthquake that struck the Bay Area on October 21. A wooden church of Norman Gothic style replaced the historic edifice, and served the parish for many years. In 1965, a new parish church was built.

In 1973, pastor Father John Williams announced his intention to rebuild the original mission church that had been destroyed in 1868. With an assist from Harry Downie, he formed the Committee for the Restoration of Mission San Jose. The project picked up steam in 1977, when California historian Father William Abeloe became pastor of St. Joseph's following the untimely death of Father Williams. An architect was hired, Gilbert A. Sanchez of San Jose, and later, contractor Frank Portman, Jr. of the Frank Portman Construction Company was hired to do the work. On July 11, 1985, the new church was dedicated.

Bishop Francisco Garcia Diego y Moreno

Bishop Cummins at native ceremony at the Ohlone Cemetery, 1992; the Cemetery had been returned to the Ohlone by Bishop Begin in 1965

IN THE ARCHDIOCESE OF SAN FRANCISCO

In the same year, gold was discovered at Sutter's Mill near Sacramento and the Gold Rush was unleashed. Thousands of argonauts flooded California from all over the world, transforming California in the process. By September 1850, California was admitted to statehood in the United States. Though California was now a United States territory, the Church in the Bay Area remained under the jurisdiction of a Mexican administrator, who resided in Santa Barbara, and remained in a diocese that included Baja California, a Mexican territory. The general disarray caused by the gold rush necessitated that an American bishop be appointed to try to provide some order for the Church in the Bay Area. Numerous letters were sent from San Francisco to the Archbishop of Baltimore (the unofficial head of the Church in the United States) requesting that an American Bishop be appointed for California. Gonzalez Rubio repeatedly petitioned Rome to create a new diocese and appoint a bishop.

Their wishes were granted in November 1849 when Dominican Charles Pius Montgomery was appointed the first bishop of the new diocese of Monterey. He quickly declined the appointment.

Life changed dramatically in the Bay Area in 1848. In that year, the state of California was formally ceded to the United States in the Treaty of Guadalupe Hidalgo, which ended the Mexican War.

Rome next looked to another Dominican to head up the new diocese. In June 1850, Spanish-born Joseph Sadoc Alemany, OP, was informed by Cardinal Giacomo Franzoni that he was to be the new Bishop of Monterey. Alemany, who had served for several years in the missions of Kentucky, Ohio, and Tennessee, was no more enthusiastic about going to California than Montgomery had been. He wrote in his diary, "June 11. Cardinal Franzoni tells me that I am bishop of Monterey and that I should prepare for consecration. No!" After consultation with his confessor, Alemany also decided to decline the appointment, but Pope Pius IX would hear none of it. In an audience on June 16, Pope Pius told Alemany, "You <u>must</u> go to California...[W]here others are drawn by gold, you must carry the Cross." Alemany was consecrated "Bishop of Monterey, Upper California" on June 30, 1850, by Cardinal Franzoni in the basilica of San Carlos al Corso in Rome. Three years later, on July 29, 1853, Rome established the Archdiocese of San Francisco, and appointed Alemany its first archbishop. The Diocese of Monterey was made a suffragan see of San Francisco with its boundaries extending from south of San Jose to the Mexican border.

The archdiocese covered the entire northern part of the state.

For the next 109 years, the area of what became the Diocese of Oakland was part of the Archdiocese of San Francisco, and was served by the following archbishops:

• Joseph Sadoc Alemany, OP, 1853-1884
• Patrick William Riordan, 1884-1914
• Edward Joseph Hanna, 1915-1934
• John Joseph Mitty, 1935-1961

At the time of the establishment of the Archdiocese, Catholic life in the East Bay was almost non-existent, as Alameda and Contra Costa Counties remained largely agricultural and sparsely settled. Oakland had less than 2,000 residents. Mission San Jose provided the only regular Catholic services; St. Mary's of the Immaculate Conception had just been established as a mission in Oakland, and Father Maximiano Agurto offered Mass and the sacraments at a number of the local ranchos.

Population growth was slow as the area was dominated by farming and ranching, though some industries such as flour and saw mills, tanneries, and fisheries, did develop, as did mining. Real growth in the East Bay began with the completion of the transcontinental railroad, which selected Oakland as its terminus. The arrival of the Central Pacific led to the rapid expansion of Oakland and other outlying areas. Oakland jumped from a community of 2,000 in 1868, to 10,500 in 1870, to 35,000 in 1880, making it the second largest city in the state. Parish life followed suit. While only four parishes existed as of 1869, by 1880 eight additional parishes and four missions had been established in the East Bay.

The tragic earthquake and fire that hit the Bay Area on April 18, 1906, devastated San Francisco, but did relatively little damage to

Archbishop Joseph S. Alemany, OP

Archbishop Patrick W. Riordan

Archbishop Edward J. Hanna

Archbishop John J. Mitty

Oakland and the East Bay towns. Many refugees fled San Francisco, and once again Oakland grew dramatically. In 1900 the population was 66,960; by 1910 the city more than doubled to 150, 174. Parishes once again grew apace. Fourteen parishes and five missions were established in Alameda and Contra Costa Counties the decade following the earthquake.

The growth of the two counties presented enormous problems for the Church in the East Bay as it strove to provide the basics of church life. The most pressing need was workers. While many lay people provided the benefactions and labor for the development of church life, much of the work of institution building fell on the backs of the clergy, and on the communities of men and women religious.

BUILDERS

The Need for Clergy

One of the most pressing problems that confronted Archbishop Alemany was the need for a competent clergy. When he arrived in California there were not enough priests, and the ones that were here were not always of the highest caliber.

Alemany lamented "California has suffered too much from the bad example of some Spanish, Irish and French clergy." And later he complained of "the dreadfully bitter cup of affliction from scandals that I have been obliged to drink." To correct this, Alemany imported a large number of priests from Ireland, especially from All Hallows Missionary College in Dublin. The East Bay would also benefit from a stream of priests from Portugal, to serve the ever growing Portuguese population. These were stopgap measures at best. Alemany wanted to erect his own seminary to produce a native clergy. In 1853, he opened a rude seminary at the old Mission Dolores that he named St. Thomas Aquinas that struggled from its inception. It was closed in 1865. Undeterred, Alemany attempted to open another seminary in 1883, this time in the East Bay. He constructed a large three-story building on the property of Mission San Jose, and invited the Marist Fathers from France to staff the new seminary. Once again placed under the patronage of St. Thomas Aquinas, this effort was an immediate fiasco. Alemany's successor, Patrick Riordan closed the seminary in 1885. The Archdiocese would wait until 1898 to establish a successful seminary, St. Patrick's at Menlo Park, which as of 2002,

St. Thomas Seminary at Mission San Jose (Courtesy of Mission San Jose Dominicans Archives)

continues to train priests for the Archdiocese and for the Diocese of Oakland.

The Dominicans

Alemany was accompanied on his trip to California by fellow Dominicans Francisco Vilarrasa and Sister Mary Goemaere. Goemaere established the first order of women religious in the state at Monterey in 1850, and Vilarrasa established the first house for Dominican men in Monterey as well. When the Archdiocese was formed in 1853, the Dominicans found themselves situated outside the archdiocese, so both orders moved to Benicia. The Dominican men soon took responsibility for evangelizing across the Strait of Carquinez in Contra Costa County. In 1854, the Dominicans built a mission church in Martinez, that they served by taking a ferry across the Strait. In 1873, St. Catherine's achieved regular parish status, with Dominican James Henry Aerden appointed the first resident pastor. In 1864, Father Vincent Vinyes, OP, who was ministering to Martinez, was called to the Empire Mine near Antioch to provide spiritual sustenance to an injured miner. He took the occasion to gather all of the local Catholics together and the mission of Most Holy Rosary in Antioch was born. In 1874, it achieved full parish status. The Dominicans evangelized the entire area. Dominican historian Fabian S. Parmisano notes that Dominicans, besides taking care of Martinez and Antioch tended the following missions: St.Michael's, Pacheco; St. Patrick's, Sommersville; Queen of All Saints (Todos los Santos), Concord; St. Patrick's, Port Costa; St. Peter Martyr, Pittsburg; St. Mary's, Walnut Creek; St. Rose's in Valona, (later, Crockett); and St. Frances of Rome, Port Chicago. By the 1920s, all of the missions and parishes were turned over to diocesan clergy except Antioch and Pittsburg, the latter receiving regular parish status in 1914.

The Dominicans increased their presence in the diocese in 1931 when they purchased land in North Oakland, near Berkeley, on which to move their House of Studies. In 1932 St. Albert's College and Priory was opened.

The Sisters of the Holy Names

The Sisters of the Holy Names from Hochelaga, Canada, pioneered Catholic educational efforts in Oakland, establishing their first convent in the city in 1868. The Sisters had been invited to

St. Catherine's in Martinez (lower right) overlooking the Carquinez Strait

come to Oakland by Father Michael King, who in 1865 had been appointed pastor of the Church of the Immaculate Conception (St. Mary's). At the time of his appointment, St. Mary's was the only parish in the entire city, and though Oakland had less than 2,000 residents, King foresaw a great future for the city. After King obtained a promise that the Sisters would come to Oakland, he set about the construction of their convent. He chose a site at some distance from the parish on the northwest shore of what eventually became Lake Merritt. At the time, the location was considered to be the middle of nowhere. King's parishioners refused to support his plan to establish the Sisters out in "the wilderness where only squirrels, rabbits, and deer abound." Undeterred, King raised money by sponsoring a lottery on his horse and his watch, with which he purchased building materials. He began construction aided by one layman, Patrick Scully. King's parishioners however,

*Father Michael King,
pastor of St. Mary's in Oakland,
1865-1904*

quickly joined his efforts when they saw their pastor working like a "common laborer." Soon the first convent, a two-story, 42'by30' building, was completed.

Six Sisters bound for Oakland, led by Sister Mary Salome, left Montreal in early 1868, going first to New York City, and then to Panama, where they crossed the isthmus, before arriving by boat in San Francisco, early Sunday morning, May 10, 1868. Since Father King was saying Mass in Oakland, he was unable to greet the Sisters. They were welcomed by the Sisters of Mercy, who hosted the Sisters at St. Mary's Hospital. Tradition has it that they were served a wonderful luncheon that included delicious California strawberries. Father King, who had arrived for the luncheon, cried "Wait, you cannot eat strawberries without cream. Give me a pitcher." From that year forward the Sisters have celebrated "Founder's Day" with strawberries and cream.

Holy Name Sisters Mary Augustine and Mary Celeste with students at May Day Picnic at Lake Merritt, 1870 (Courtesy of Oakland Public History Room)

Two days later, Father King took the Sisters to their new convent. The Sisters were to open a "select school" at the convent, while at the same time conducting a free parochial school, St. Aloysius, attached to St. Mary's parish. Two sisters would travel each day to the school. The grounds of the new convent were described by one sister, "The grounds are quite wild yet, barren would be a better word, one small knot of rose bushes blooming in the front garden." Nonetheless, the Convent of Our Lady of the Sacred Heart was dedicated by Archbishop Alemany on May 22, 1868, and the school opened with five students.

The first class graduated in 1872, making it the first high school graduation in the city of Oakland. In 1880, a college was opened, but only women preparing for the sisterhood were admitted. In 1908, the school took the name College of the Holy Names, and in 1916, the college was opened to regular students.

The fortunes of the Sisters were directed largely by their second superior, Mother Jean Baptiste, who arrived later in 1868 as a "sub-assistant" to the General Superior of the Order. Mother John Baptist served as superior in Oakland until 1877, when she was made first provincial superior, and in 1886, she became superior general of the entire community.

College of the Holy Names

View of Lake Merritt from College of the Holy Names

The Sisters provided extraordinary service to what would become the Diocese of Oakland. Besides their initial foundation, the Sisters eventually staffed seven additional parochial elementary schools: Sacred Heart (1880), St. Francis de Sales (1887), St. Augustine (1918), Our Lady of Lourdes (1924), Holy Spirit, Fremont (1956), St. Theresa (1958), and St. Bede in Hayward (1964). In addition, in 1931 they opened Holy Names Central High School in the Oakland Hills. The College continued to prosper and in 1957, the Sisters moved to the beautiful present location on Mountain Blvd. The old site was purchased by Henry J. Kaiser, and the Kaiser Center built on the former convent grounds.

The Christian Brothers

The Christian Brothers came to San Francisco in 1868, after Alemany had pleaded with the order for more than a decade to send brothers. [This section is based on Brother Ronald Isetti's, FSC, excellent history, *Called to the Pacific*.] In 1862, Alemany had established St. Mary's College in San Francisco to provide undergraduate education for prospective seminarians. The college struggled until it was taken over by the Christian Brothers. Eight brothers were sent from New York, under the leadership of Brother

St. Mary's College on 30th and Broadway in Oakland, affectionately called "The Old Brickpile." (Courtesy of Christian Brothers Archives)

Justin McMahon, arriving on August 10, 1868. The Brothers quickly revitalized the school. They made their first establishment in Oakland in 1870, by moving their novitiate to 5th and Webster, where they also established St. Joseph's Academy, a grammar and high school. In 1879, the novitiate moved to Martinez. Soon grapevines were planted, from which the Christian Brothers Winery would evolve.

In 1879, Brother Justin was replaced by his stepbrother, Brother Bettelin McMahon. Brother

Bettelin began to look into the possibility of moving the college to Oakland. The Brothers had long disliked the foggy, cold climate of San Francisco, which they thought unhealthy for their student body. In 1883, the Brothers purchased eight acres in the Broadway area of Oakland, which was described at the time as the "suburbs of Oakland." In 1889, a five-story building, which came to be known affectionately as "the Old Brickpile," was finished and the college moved to Oakland. The 1896-97 College catalogue sang the praises of Oakland for "the climate is mild and healthful, the surrounding scenery delightful…"

Prior to moving the college to Oakland, the Brothers took over a series of parochial schools in Oakland, which they intended to serve as feeders for their high schools and college: St. Anthony (1880), St. Mary (1881), St. Patrick (1884), Sacred Heart (1886), and St. Francis de Sales (1889). Unfortunately for the Brothers, they would withdraw from all these schools between 1900 and 1915, as a result of a shortage of brothers, but more importantly, because pastors found their services too expensive, and preferred the cheaper labor of the women religious. Nonetheless, the Brothers persevered in their high school and college ministry.

By the mid-1920s the College was bursting at the seams. To provide more space, the college's high school department was split off and moved to Berkeley. It was merged with St. Joseph's Academy, which had moved to Berkeley in 1903. Together a new school was formed, named Saint Mary's College High School.

Even with this the College needed more room, so in 1927 ground was broken for a new campus in Moraga, and the campus was moved once more in 1928, again to what was considered the middle of nowhere. Once in Moraga the school entered what was considered

Sister of Mercy with students at our Lady of Lourdes Academy at St. Anthony's parish (Courtesy of Sisters of Mercy Archives)

its "Golden Age." Under the direction of renowned lecturer Brother Leo Meehan, St. Mary's demonstrated a renewed academic and intellectual vigor. At the same time (actually beginning in the 1920s), it was earning national accolades for its football program under Edward P. "Slip" Madigan. Only the record winning streak of the Brothers' De LaSalle High School's football team in the 1990s could match the passion stirred by Madigan's "Galloping Gaels."

For more than 130 years, the Brothers have provided superb service to the Diocese of Oakland.

Sisters of Mercy

The Sisters of Mercy came to the Archdiocese of San Francisco from Ireland in 1854, led by the dynamic, young superior, Mother M. Baptist Russell. The Sisters' name became synonymous with charity as they shortly established St. Mary's Hospital (1861), a magdalen asylum, a home for the aged poor (1871), and other institutions of charity. The Sisters were also educators, establishing their first school in San Francisco in 1871. In 1877 they came to Oakland, where they began Our Lady of Lourdes Academy in St. Anthony's parish in East Oakland (called Brooklyn at the time). As the Mercy history

recounts it, "On July 2, 1877 Mother Russell brought seven Sisters of Mercy to begin a school in the wide open spaces" of Oakland. The school served the community until 1931 when it was closed. From St. Anthony's, the Sisters taught catechism in a number of the local parishes.

The Sisters are better known in the East Bay for their work with the elderly. In 1871, they established a home for the aged on Rincon Hill in San Francisco, next to St. Mary's Hospital. The earthquake of 1906 devastated the building and forced an evacuation of the residents to Oakland. The Sisters were aided by the legendary Father Peter C. Yorke, pastor of St. Anthony's, who assisted in finding shelter and relief. Fortunately, the Sisters had purchased five acres of land in the Fruitvale district of Oakland in 1893. They decided to rebuild there, and the new Our Lady's Home was dedicated on March 17, 1908. Over the next nine decades, Our Lady's Home continued to expand its facilities and services for the elderly, opening Serra Senior Center in 1961. In 1984, Our Lady's Home was renamed Mercy Retirement and Care Center.

The Mercies would be joined in their service to the elderly by the Little Sisters of the Poor. In 1901, the Little Sisters opened St. Anne's

Home for the Aged in San Francisco. In 1913, they journeyed across the Bay to establish St. Joseph's Home for the Aged, which served the diocese until 1979.

The Sisters of the Presentation

Like the Mercies, the Sisters of the Presentation came to San Francisco from Ireland in 1854. In 1855, Mothers M. Teresa Comerford and M. Xavier Daly established the foundation of the Presentations on the West Coast. The Sisters quickly earned a reputation for being out-standing educators. By the early 1870s, they were teaching close to one-third of the students in Catholic schools in San Francisco.

In the mid-1870s the Sisters began to look for a foundation outside of San Francisco that would enjoy a better climate. In their first twelve years in San Francisco, twelve sisters, including several young ones, had died of consumption. Mother Teresa chose Berkeley as three Irish

Catholic farmers offered her a substantial grant of land in the city if she built a school there. Thus, Mother accepted the offer of a parcel of land from James McGee, on the "plains of Berkeley," not too distant from the recently established University of California. Before any Catholic parish or church was located in Berkeley, the cornerstone was laid for the Presentation Convent and school in 1877. Mass was offered in the newly completed chapel of the convent on Christmas Day, 1877, for the Catholics of Berkeley.

Eight sisters arrived from San Francisco on June 27, 1878, and the first community Mass was celebrated on June 28, the feast of the Sacred Heart. St. Joseph's Presentation Convent was dedicated two days later. Regular Mass for the locals was offered in the convent school rooms, served by priests from neighboring Sacred Heart parish in Oakland.

It soon became evident that a resident priest was necessary. Mother Teresa wrote her brother, the Very Reverend Pierce M. Comerford, who was then convalescing in Ireland, urging him to come to Berkeley. Father Comerford had provided distinguished service for more than thirty years as

St. Joseph's Home for the Aged, Oakland

Elderly gentlemen relax at Our Lady's Home in Oakland (Courtesy of Sisters of Mercy Archives)

a missionary priest in Mauritius, before his health forced him to return to Ireland. At his sister's request, he came to Berkeley on October 9, 1878 and was appointed assistant pastor at Sacred Heart with responsibility for the Catholics in Berkeley and the convent. In April 1879, St. Joseph's Parish was established, and Comerford appointed its first pastor. Mass continued to be offered in the classrooms of the convent. In 1881, he opened a school for boys also tended by the Sisters. Unfortunately, his sister died before the end of the year.

By then the Sisters were conducting a grammar school for girls, one for boys, and a high school for girls. The Sisters had served for more than a century when the Presentation High School was closed in 1988. The elementary school continues under lay leadership.

Sisters of Notre Dame de Namur

The Sisters of Notre Dame came to the Bay Area prior to the establishment of the Archdiocese, beginning Notre Dame Academy in 1851 in San Jose. In 1873, St. Joseph's in Alameda was opened as a mission of St. Anthony's parish in Oakland. By 1881, Alameda had some 6,000 residents and St. Anthony's pastor, Father William Gleeson, believed the town was ready for a school. On March 27, 1881 four Notre Dame Sisters led by Sister Marie de Sacre Coeur arrived in Alameda and opened Notre Dame Academy the following day. The first thirty-seven students may have seemed an unpromising lot as the historian of St. Joseph's described them, "They were 'uncouth as could be found,'[one Sister wrote], and summing up their ignorance, she added that most of them had never heard of the Creation, much less the Deluge." Nonetheless, the Sisters persevered. The parish was formally established in 1885. In 1935, a boys' high school, St. Joseph's was opened under the direction of the Marianist Brothers and in 1985, the two schools merged to form St. Joseph's-Notre Dame High School.

Sisters of St. Joseph of Carondelet

In 1883, Father John B. McNally, the founding pastor of St. Patrick's Parish in West Oakland, wrote to Mother Agatha Guthrie of the Sisters of St. Joseph of Carondelet, after she had

Presentation Sisters with students in Berkeley; St. Joseph's parish church in background (Courtesy of Sisters of Presentation Archives)

agreed to send Sisters to staff his parish school: "I understand now that your order will send a community to this parish, without any expense to me, ready, able, active, energetic, zealous and ardent in the fervor of God." The Sisters turned out to be all these things. They arrived in late December 1883, and on January 1, 1884, St. Joseph's Institute was opened with approximately 200 children. (In 1932, the school was renamed St. Patrick's School.) The community prospered under the leadership of its first superior and school principal, Mother Florence Benigna Reilly. One Sister wrote to St. Louis that the Sisters were well pleased with Oakland, "Here we see nothing but sunshine and flowers—everything green and springlike... St. Patrick's Church presents a fine appearance and the

Dominican Sisters Agatha Watts and Benedicta Kroutsch travel in style, 1903

Sisters' residence is one of the most cosy and at the same time respectable houses in the neighborhood...The prospects are very bright here for a large school." The Sister's assessment was correct and the school expanded rapidly.

The Sisters' contribution to Oakland did not end with St. Patrick's. In 1895, the Sisters took over direction of the newly formed St. Joseph's Home for Deaf Mutes. In 1930, they accepted

direction of St. Jarlath's elementary school. And between 1948 and 1967, they staffed seven grade schools and one high school in the diocese: Queen of All Saints, Concord (1948); St. Catherine, Martinez (1949); Santa Maria, Orinda (1960); Christ the King, Pleasant Hill (1961); St. Perpetua, Lafayette (1963); St. Francis of Assisi, Concord; St. Agnes, Concord (1967); and Carondelet High School (1965).

In 1994, Carondelet Sister Barbara Flannery became the first female Chancellor in the history of the diocese.

Mission San Jose Dominicans

In 1876, three Dominican sisters, led by Mother Pia Backes, only twenty four years old at the time, came from Brooklyn, New York, to establish the Dominican Congregation of the Queen of the Holy Rosary in San Francisco, a place she considered "a foreign land". As the Order's roots were German, the Sisters were given the care of the German Catholic school at St. Boniface. In 1883, they established Immaculate Conception Academy in the Mission District of San Francisco.

In 1890, Archbishop Patrick Riordan offered to sell the former Seminary at Mission San Jose to the Dominicans. Mother Pia prayed over the decision, hesitating due to the enormous expense that would be incurred. She initially planned on establishing a school for Native Americans, but this never materialized. Instead, on February 25, 1891 she decided to purchase the land and open a boarding school. Mother Pia banked on the grapes and olives that came with the purchase of the land to support the venture: "The grape crop will probably pay the interest, and the olive crop, the capital. The board will support the house." On January 4, 1892, a school dedicated to St. Joseph and known as the Josephinum was opened. By 1894, enrollment was so poor that the Josephinum was transformed into an orphanage. In 1910, the orphanage was moved up the street and renamed St. Mary's of the Palms. In 1893, the Dominicans had expanded their presence in the East Bay by establishing St. Elizabeth's Elementary School in Oakland.

In 1906, the Motherhouse and novitiate were moved from San Francisco to the grounds at Mission San Jose. Thus, the Sisters came to be known as the Mission San Jose Dominicans. By 1964, the Sisters were teaching in five elementary schools in the Diocese of Oakland, plus St. Elizabeth's High School.

Sisters of Providence

By 1901, Oakland had grown to the point that Archbishop Riordan believed it was time to establish a Catholic hospital in Oakland. He appealed to the Sisters of Providence of Montreal, who had already supplied such outstanding medical service in Washington and Oregon, to open a hospital in Oakland. The Sisters agreed. By January 1902, they had purchased a large lot at the corner of Broadway and 26th Streets in the heart of Oakland. The Hospital was incorporated in 1903, and the new hospital building completed and dedicated on

April 4, 1904. The same year a school of nursing was opened, a school that operated until 1972. The founding Sisters were led by Mother Mary Theresa, who oversaw the hospital until 1909.

The Sisters provided extraordinary service, particularly during the tragic aftermath of the earthquake of 1906, and again during the influenza epidemic of 1918. In 1926, a new hospital building was opened at 30th and Summit streets. The third Providence hospital was completed in 1979. In 1991, Providence merged with Merritt Hospital to form Summit Hospital.

Almost six decades after the establishment of Providence in 1960, the Sisters of St. Joseph's of Wichita were invited to open the second Catholic hospital in Alameda County. On October 22, 1962, St. Rose Hospital in Hayward was opened, and was dedicated on May 24, 1963 by Bishop Floyd Begin.

First Providence Hospital, Oakland, 1904 (Courtesy of Oakland Public History Room)

Mother Pia Backes with her Mission San Jose Dominican sisters (Courtesy of Mission San Jose Dominicans Archives)

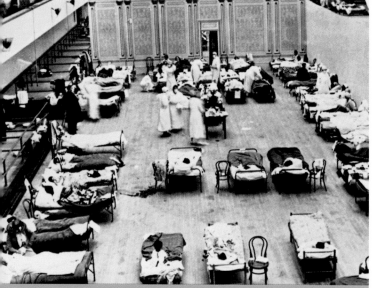

Providence Sisters tending the sick during the 1918 influenza epidemic, at the Oakland Civic Center

The Paulists and the Newman Club

On December 8, 1899, the Catholic students at the University of California at Berkeley gathered to form a Newman Club. Shortly thereafter, Father John J. Cantwell, assistant pastor at St. Joseph's in Berkeley, was appointed the group's chaplain. (Cantwell went on to a distinguished career, first as Archbishop Riordan's secretary, and later as Archbishop of Los Angeles). In 1906, Archbishop Riordan sought the services of the Paulist Fathers to staff the Newman Center. The Paulists had made their first establishment outside of New York in 1894, when they came to staff the old St. Mary's Cathedral in San Francisco. The Paulists agreed to send a chaplain, and in 1907, Father Thomas Verner Moore, who later became the leading Catholic psychologist in the United States, took over as chaplain. Riordan purchased a house on Ridge Road, north of the campus, to serve as the club's center. He also purchased an adjoining lot to construct a more substantial building. The first Mass celebrated by Moore was on August 26, 1907. In 1908, Riordan donated $40,000 from a burse given to him on the occasion of his twenty-fifth episcopal anniversary to the construction of a new center. The new building, an impressive three-story structure that included a "lecture hall, library, recreation rooms, and a striking, vaulted chapel," was dedicated on March 10, 1910 and named after St. Thomas Aquinas. The center served the students for the next fifty-seven years.

In 1965, Bishop Begin broke ground for a new Newman Center on the south side of campus. The new center was to incorporate the Newman Club into regular parish life, and Holy Spirit Newman parish was created. In May 1967, the new church and complex, designed by architect Mario Ciampi were dedicated, and the new Newman apostolate begun.

Berkeley Newman Club

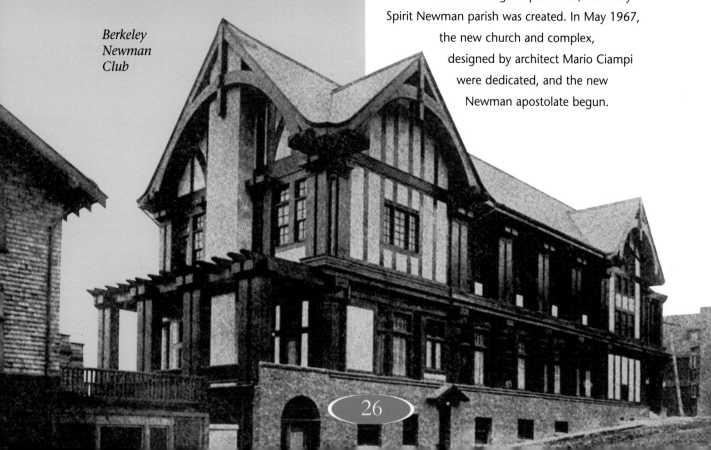

The Sisters of the Holy Family

The Sisters of the Holy Family are the only order still in existence to originate in the Archdiocese of San Francisco. The order was established November 6, 1872 in San Francisco by Elizabeth Armer, who would eventually take the name Mother Dolores. Lizzie, as she was known, was born in Australia in 1850, and emigrated to the United States with her family. When she was nine, her mother died, and so Lizzie was placed in the home of Mary and Richard Tobin of Hibernia Bank fame. In the late 1860s, she became acquainted with Father John J. Prendergast, the rector of the Cathedral parish in San Francisco, where she taught catechism and decorated the altar. Prendergast became her life-long advisor, and is considered a co-founder of the Holy Family Sisters.

Lizzie decided to enter a contemplative order, but Archbishop Alemany told her, "Father Prendergast and I have another work for you." At their request Lizzie joined with two other young women to found the Sisters of the Holy Family. Her initial two companions fell by the wayside, but in 1874, she was joined by Ellen O'Connor, who became the second permanent member of the congregation. They were officially recognized as a religious congregation on September 10, 1878.

Two of the Sisters' basic ministries, according to historian Sr. Michaela O'Connor, SHF, were to provide day homes for the children of working

Foundress of Holy Family Sisters, Mother Dolores (Courtesy of Holy Family Sisters Archives)

St. Vincent's Day Home, Oakland (Courtesy of St. Vincent's Day Home)

Holy Family Sisters on way to vacation school: they became known as "The nuns who drive" (Courtesy of Holy Family Sisters Archives)

parents, and to provide religious education for Catholic children attending public schools. Over the years this latter ministry has become the one most closely associated with the Holy Family Sisters.

By 1911, the Sisters were already operating several day homes in San Francisco, and looked to expand to Oakland. Mother Dolores's successor, Mother M. Teresa O'Connor, selected a site at 8th Street and Chestnut in Oakland. Placed under the direction of Sister M. Gertrude, St. Vincent's Day Home was dedicated on October 2, 1911, and opened on October 16. The convent annals record, "the first children received were twin boys of three and a half years. The father, a Catholic, was sick in the hospital, the mother, a Protestant, was working in San Francisco. The children were baptized Catholics. They lived in Alameda and were brought to the home by the mother on her way to work." By November, eight sisters were taking care of 80 children, of all nationalities—"Irish, German, American, Italian, Portuguese, Slavonian, French, Swedish and Scottish."

The Sisters also began to teach Sunday School, first at St. Louis Bertrand in Oakland, and eventually all over Alameda and Contra Costa Counties. The Sisters became the backbone of CCD programs throughout the diocese.

In 1948, the Sisters purchased a large plot of land in Mission San Jose known as the Palmdale Estates, and in 1949, they moved their novitiate there. In 1959, they moved their Motherhouse there from San Francisco to a newly erected complex.

The Redemptorists

The Redemptorists came to Oakland in the early 1920s, establishing Holy Redeemer College as a minor seminary for their West Coast Province.

In the early 1930s, they purchased land in Livermore, where they established Villa San Clemente, a Mission House for the province. From here the Redemptorists supplied "parish missionaries" throughout the East Bay. The parish mission was a week of intensive sermons and prayer designed to revitalize the faith of the local parish communities. The Redemptorists became known for their superb preaching and personal warmth. In the 1960s, the seminary was closed but the facility was transformed into Holy Redeemer Center which has been a center of prayer, reflection and renewal, ever since.

The Immigrant Church

While the religious orders did a good deal of the institution building and ministry, the Church in Alameda and Contra Counties had a decidedly cosmopolitan air about it. In short, the church was an immigrant church. Four immigrant groups made up the bulk of the Catholic population: the Irish, the Portuguese, the Germans, and the Italians.

The Irish were the largest group extending throughout the two counties from the Irish farmers of Berkeley and Dublin to the urban, working class in Oakland. Parish registers throughout the diocese are filled with Irish names as are the rosters of priests and Sisters of the diocese. Of all the Irish, however, one in particular stands out, Father Peter C. Yorke. Yorke, who is the most famous priest in the history of the Archdiocese, served as pastor of St. Anthony's in Oakland from 1903 to 1913. He obtained legendary status among Bay Area Catholics for his prominent role in a number of conflicts and developments. First, as editor of the archdiocesan newspaper, *The Monitor*, during the 1890s, he vanquished the anti-Catholic American Protective Association in San Francisco through public debate and exposes published in *The Monitor*, a crusade he brought to Oakland in 1897. During this conflict Yorke developed his acerbic rhetorical style, castigating his opponents in most unflattering (and unpriestly) language. Second, he emerged as spiritual leader and chief publicist for the union during the great Teamsters Strike of 1901. Yorke placed the Church in the Bay Area squarely on the side of labor, and enjoyed widespread respect and admiration from union leaders and rank and file as a labor priest. Third, he founded and edited a local Irish newspaper, *The Leader*, in 1902, which gave him a platform to discuss and publicize his views on various local issues, political and otherwise. Fourth, he published a series of *Textbooks of Religion*, that adapted the Baltimore Catechism to appropriate grade levels. These texts were adopted and used throughout the archdiocese and elsewhere. Fifth, Yorke vigorously supported the fight for a free Irish state, particularly supporting the efforts of Eamon de Valera. Yorke was the preeminent Irishman in the Bay Area.

The Portuguese represented the second largest group in the diocese. Portuguese immigrants were present from the earliest days of California but did not start arriving in large numbers until the 1880s. They settled largely in Oakland and in the Hayward—Fremont area, where they worked primarily in farming, ranching, and in the canneries. The majority of the Portuguese immigrants to the Bay Area came from the Azores.

The first parish to work predominantly with the Portuguese was Holy Ghost parish in Centerville (Fremont). Portuguese Father Dominic Governo was appointed first pastor in 1886. In 1887, on the feast of Pentecost, the parish initiated what became an annual Portuguese religious celebration, the Holy Ghost Festival. The celebration has its origin in the fourteenth century, when the Azores islanders were saved

Father Peter C. Yorke, center, with Archbishop Riordan, right, at St. Anthony's Oakland, 1912

St. Joseph's Portuguese Parish, Confirmation 1939, Bishop Thomas Connolly with Father Charles Philipps

from famine through the intercession of the Holy Spirit. When Queen St. Isabella learned of the miraculous intervention, she organized a solemn procession in honor of the Holy Ghost. Accompanied by her maids, she carried her crown through the streets of Lisbon to the cathedral, where she left her crown in thanksgiving to the Holy Ghost. The annual celebration at Holy Spirit parish re-enacts the queen's procession. Processions also came to be celebrated in Newark and other Portuguese centers. In 1954, a report from San Francisco to the apostolic delegate concluded, "The Holy Ghost celebrations…have done a great deal to help to preserve the faith among the Portuguese emigrants."

Ministry to the Portuguese began around 1890 in Oakland with Father John Tavares ministering to the community. In 1892, a Portuguese National parish, St. Joseph's, was established, with Father John Fernandes serving as first pastor. In 1902, the parish was turned over to the Salesian Fathers, who had come to San Francisco in 1897. By 1915, a large community had formed in East Oakland, so another Portuguese National parish, Mary Help of Christians was established, also placed under the care of the Salesians.

In August 1936, the Portuguese community celebrated the visit of the Patriarch of Lisbon, Cardinal Emmanuel Concalves Cerejeira to commemorate the sixth centenary of the death of St. Isabella, Queen of Portugal. 12,000 attended his Pontifical Mass at the Oakland Civic Auditorium. He offered Compline and Benediction at the Cathedral and was feted to a banquet by Archbishop John J. Mitty at the Fairmont Hotel. A Portuguese pastor concluded, "All these things had a tremendous influence for good among the Portuguese people."

The next major immigrant group was the Germans. Germans began settling in Oakland, particularly in the Fruitvale area. By 1900, over 6,000 Germans lived in Alameda County. In 1892, the Franciscan Fathers, who were responsible for the German parish in San Francisco, established a German National parish in Fruitvale, St. Elizabeth's. Though the parish became a territorial parish in 1906, it retained a German flavor.

St. Elizabeth's First Communion 1912 (Courtesy of Oakland Public History Room)

Italians were scattered throughout the diocese in fishing and other industries. The Salesians, who took care of the Italians in San Francisco, also began ministering to the Italians in Oakland from St. Joseph's and Mary Help of Christians. By 1932, both parishes were designated as national parishes for Portuguese <u>and</u> Italians.

Traditional Societies

Catholic societies flourished in the East Bay. Several societies founded in San Francisco were also established in Oakland. In 1885, the Young Men's Institute and in 1889, the Young Ladies Institute were established in Oakland. Both organizations became significant organizations in the diocese. In 1895, the League of the Cross Cadets, a temperance organization organized along military lines, came to Oakland, as did the Knights of Columbus in 1903. The Italian Catholic Federation, founded in San Francisco by Luigi Providenza and Father A. R. Bandini in 1924, was formed in Alameda and Oakland in 1926. These and other societies, too numerous to mention here, flourished in the diocese.

World War II

World War II dramatically altered the make-up of the Bay Area. Prior to 1941, a small African American community had developed largely around the railroad industry in Oakland. In 1941, however, President Franklin D. Roosevelt signed an executive order which forbade discrimination in the war industries. This set off a mass migration of African Americans from the south to California to obtain jobs in shipbuilding and other war industries. The result was the enormous growth of the African American community in Oakland and Richmond. By 1960, the African American population made up close to 35% of the city of Oakland.

As African Americans moved in, many of the older ethnic groups moved out, presenting the church with a major problem. Since African Americans were more than 90% Protestant, their influx meant that some parishes might suffer a large drop in membership. In 1950, a special priests' committee cautioned that St. Andrew's, St. Patrick's, St. Joseph's, St. Mary's, and St. Columba's in Oakland, and St. Mark's in

Richmond, would soon be in neighborhoods largely African American, and thus "an increasing number of churches will become empty unless the Negroes have been converted." Their report was remarkably forward looking, arguing that to "create a climate for conversions," priests should become involved in the civil rights struggle, making "the voice of the church heard on basic human rights...It should give a clear cut policy on housing, slum clearance and integration, and these should be constantly reiterated." The priests were realistic, however, acknowledging that the biggest obstacle to conversion was "Prejudice among our own, lack of charity, and a patronizing attitude."

On the positive side, in 1941, a branch of the Knights of St. Peter Claver at St. Patrick's Parish in West Oakland was established under the leadership of William J. Knox. Three months later, the Ladies Auxiliary was founded by Rose Casanave; Rose went on to become one of the outstanding Catholic laywomen in the diocese. Bishop Begin dubbed her "the patron saint of the Black Catholic Movement in the Bay Area." The Knights are a fraternal, social and charitable organization founded in 1909 by several prominent African American laymen under the auspices of the Josephite Fathers, in Mobile, Alabama. Sad to say, the organization was necessary because the Knights of Columbus resisted integration efforts. By the end of the 1950s, branches of the Knights and Ladies had been established at three additional Oakland parishes: St. Joseph's, St. Columba, and St. Louis Bertrand. They continue to play a vital role in the diocese as of 2002.

The war years also witnessed an increased migration of Mexicans to the Bay Area. A small community had developed in Oakland during the 1920s, with ministry provided by St. Joseph's and Mary Help of Christians where the Salesians supplied a Spanish-speaking priest. In 1932, the two parishes were designated national parishes for the Portuguese, the Italians and the Mexicans.

During World War II, the U.S. initiated the bracero program, whereby Mexican nationals were brought to California to work in the fields, then returned to Mexico. Regular immigration also increased, and many of the new arrivals found work in the fields. Prior to the 1940s, little was done in terms of ministry to the migrant workers and the braceros. In 1936, Father Charles Philipps, a French immigrant himself, was appointed pastor at St. Mary's in West Oakland. Philipps was an extraordinary priest who gained fame for establishing a summer camp on the Russian River called Sunshine Camp, which he staffed with seminarians, and to which he brought inner-city youth largely from Oakland. In addition, Philipps started a soup kitchen and homeless shelter in the parish. His real contribution, however, was alerting Archbishop Mitty to the growing need for ministry to the migrant workers. Philipps did what he could from St. Mary's, but in 1950, he inspired four young priests to form the Spanish Mission Band for the Archdiocese: Fathers Ralph Duggan, ordained in 1945, Donald McDonnell, Thomas McCullough, and John Garcia, all ordained in 1947. In 1956, Duggan was replaced by Father Ronald Burke, ordained in 1954. They were freed from regular parish ministry so they could go into the fields to minister to the migrant workers and braceros. The initial work was primarily spiritual; the Band began visiting migrant and bracero camps offering Mass, hearing confessions, praying the rosary, teaching catechism, and encouraging devotions. Duggan, Burke, and Garcia concentrated on Alameda and Contra Costa Counties (though McCullough later provided distinguished service as a priest in the Diocese of Oakland).

Father John Garcia gave an account of his work in 1951 in which he reported, "Lately

I have been concentrating more on the camps. Around Brentwood during peak season…there are about 1,000 men to say nothing of women and children. These are practically all Catholic and there are many more between Brentwood and Stockton…I have been going to camps in the evenings, saying the rosary, giving talks, hearing confessions, and saying Mass in the morning before they go to work. Perhaps something could be worked out with other dioceses to keep following the migratory worker. They keep moving from one diocese to the other, yet still remain Catholic and in need of a priest." Besides visiting the camps, Garcia also began home visitations. He became deeply loved, not only for his simplicity and piety, but because he never arrived empty handed—he always brought a gift of some basic foodstuff, beans, rice or flour.

As the Band visited the camps they became appalled by the living conditions they observed. As a result, the Band increasingly turned to "issues of social justice." McDonnell and McCullough in particular, began to agitate to end the bracero system and to encourage union organizing. They received permission to explain to the workers "the teachings of the Church on labor-management cooperation" as articulated in the great papal social encyclicals. Perhaps the greatest contribution the Band made was the discovery of two young Mexican-American workers, Cesar Chavez and Dolores Huerta. Huerta and Chavez went on to found the National Farmworkers Association (which later became the United Farmworkers,UFW).

The Band were the pioneers in Latino ministry that would blossom in the 1960s and 1970s in Oakland.

Displaced Priests

In the aftermath of World War II, many people fled the brutal repression that accompanied the Communist takeover of Eastern Europe. These

Father Ronald Burke blesses a bracero

immigrants were dubbed "DPs" for "displaced persons." The Diocese of Oakland benefited from the services of many "DP priests," who escaped the religious persecution occurring in places like Poland, Lithuania, Slovenia, and Yugoslavia. Several had spent time at the notorious German concentration camp at Dachau. Amazingly, each of the following priests served Catholics in the Bay Area for more than forty years, with several serving more than fifty: Monsignors Leon Degner and Leo Kristanc, Fathers John Gregov, Stefan Kopania, Wicenty Kruk, Jan Stasiak, Aloysius Zitko, Joseph Pirc, Theofilus Palis, and Vladimir Kozina.

Expansion and Growth

Alameda and Contra Counties experienced explosive growth following the war, and the Catholic Church experienced an equally amazing burst. Nineteen new parishes were established between 1945 and 1961, and three parishes were raised from mission to full parish status. Thirty-two new elementary schools were built and opened. Two new high schools were established—Bishop O'Dowd in 1951 and Salesian in 1960. Catholic life at almost every level seemed to be flourishing. In light of the vibrancy of Catholic life in Alameda and Contra Costa counties rumors began to circulate that Oakland was to become its own new diocese.

On October 15, 1961, long-time Archbishop John J. Mitty died, and a new era was about to begin.

A Parish *Family Album*

The heart of the Diocese is its parishes. The following materials have been provided by the parishes themselves, and have been compiled, organized and edited by Mary Carmen Batiza

ST. JOSEPH, FREMONT
(Mission San Jose)
(1797)

Mission Church rebuilt 1985

Mission San Jose Interior

ST. MARY, IMMACULATE CONCEPTION, OAKLAND (1853)

July 1941, Solemn Blessing of Babies which took place during annual St. Anne's Novena at St. Mary's

Laying of the cornerstone of St. Francis de Sales, 1891

The second parish in the area now known as the Diocese of Oakland, has the oldest standing church, built in 1872 by the fourth pastor, Father Michael King (1865-1904), who was also responsible for bringing the Holy Names Sisters (1868) and the Christian Brothers to Oakland to establish Catholic schools. Always diverse, the parish consisted of, first Irish, then Mexicans, and currently provides liturgies for the Filipino and Vietnamese communities along with the English liturgy. The parish has seen many changes including the incorporation of the Cathedral of St. Francis de Sales parish after the 1989 Loma Prieta Earthquake. St. Mary-St. Francis de Sales continues as a multicultural parish with a Parish Pastoral Council from the three communities; multicultural Union Liturgies several times a year; and a strong commitment to social justice issues, including a winter shelter for the homeless.

ST. LEANDER, SAN LEANDRO (1864)

Since its creation, St. Leander Parish has been a fixture in San Leandro. The Dominican Sisters of San Rafael blessed the community for 114 years with their presence and ministry to students and parishioners. Today, people from vast backgrounds—the young, the old, the poor, American, Portuguese, Latinos, Filipinos, and those who have lived all their lives in San Leandro-come joyfully praising God, to be nourished by the Lord, and offer their gifts of service.

St. Leander: Easter Vigil celebration, 2001, Father John Prochaska

ST. ANTHONY, OAKLAND (1871)

Founded in 1871, the parish was the home parish of the illustrious Father Peter C. Yorke (1903-1913). It maintains one of the oldest schools in the diocese. The parish served first Irish, Portuguese, Italians, then Mexicans, and more recently Filipinos and Vietnamese.

ST. PAUL, SAN PABLO (1869)

St. Paul's was the first parish established in Contra Costa County. It was first established as a mission in 1864 and became a full parish in 1869. Former Governor Juan Alvarado donated the land for the church. The present church, a San Pablo landmark, was built in 1931. The parish school opened in 1952.

The Conventual Franciscans have administered the parish since 1984.

The parish is now multicultural. Liturgy is celebrated in six different languages: English, Spanish, Vietnamese, Kmhmu', Portuguese, and Tagalog.

ST. CATHERINE OF SIENA, MARTINEZ
(Mission –1854; Parish –1873)

The first recorded Mass in Martinez was in 1850 and in 1854 St. Catherine of Siena became a mission of St. Dominic Parish in Benicia, staffed by the Dominican Fathers. In 1873 the mission became a parish with its first resident pastor, Father James Aerden, OP (1873-1896). Over the years, parishioners have built a cemetery, four churches, a school, three rectories, a convent and parish offices. The parish school was established in 1949, staffed by the Sisters of St. Joseph of Carondelet. At the beginning of the 21st century the community brings a strong Vatican II liturgy, extensive lay participation, a new building project and solid ties with the town of Martinez.

MOST HOLY ROSARY, ANTIOCH (1874

In 1851, a heretofore unnamed town of less than 100 was given the name of Antioch. The Catholic population was negligible, but in Benicia the Dominican Fathers were well-established and served the area including Antioch. The first Mass was celebrated in 1864. When St. Catherine of Siena became a parish, the Mission of Most Holy Rosary in Antioch came under its jurisdiction and in 1874 was established as a full parish. To minister to the needs of families in the fast growing region of Contra Costa County, a school was opened in 1955, staffed by the Dominican Sisters of San Rafael. Again, in response to local needs, a Spanish language Mass was started in 1970.

To implement the liturgical changes of Vatican II, a new church was built in the 1960s. Unfortunately in January 1987 the church was nearly destroyed by arson. It was rebuilt in the same year.

This remains a very active parish, which relies heavily on the laity for the administrative and pastoral work of the parish.

SACRED HEART, OAKLAND (1876)

Sacred Heart Parish community was established in 1876. The first members of the parish were mainly Italian, Irish and Portuguese. This closely knit community built the first church, which was dedicated by Archbishop Joseph S. Alemany on January 17, 1876. Destroyed by fire one year later, a temporary structure was built, replaced by a beautiful stone building, which was dedicated in 1902. This church was destroyed in 1989 by the Loma Prieta earthquake. In 1998 the present church was dedicated (photo at left).

Sacred Heart Parish has always been a strong community and continues to this day with a diversity of about a dozen cultural groups. Diocesan priests staffed the parish until 1991 when the Oblates of Mary Immaculate took it over. The school (1880), which was staffed by the Holy Names Sisters for almost a century, and the parish center, are the center of the lives of the parishioners.

ST. JOSEPH THE WORKER, BERKELEY (1879)

St. Joseph's Parish had its beginning, when the Sisters of the Presentation opened their school in 1878. The parish was formally inaugurated in 1879 with its first pastor, Father Pierce Comerford. Its population grew dramatically after the 1906 San Francisco earthquake. Since then it has enjoyed a long and vital history. The present name, St. Joseph the Worker, was given in the mid-1970's. It has long enjoyed a diverse and ethnically mixed population. Presently it is composed of a large Latino population. It also enjoys a wide, favorable reputation for its commitment to Social Justice.

ST. MICHAEL, LIVERMORE (1878)

Founded in 1878 to serve the Livermore Valley, a school was established in 1913 under the care of the Dominican Sisters of San Rafael. Today it is a vital, multicultural parish.

ST. PATRICK, OAKLAND (1879)

On April 6, 1879, Father J. B. McNally became the first pastor of St. Patrick Church. The parish primarily served Irish immigrants, but for most of its history it has been a multicultural community comprised of Irish, Portuguese, Yugoslavs, Italians, Latinos and African Americans.

The Sisters of St. Joseph of Carondelet established the school in 1883. The Divine Word Missionaries served the parish on and off from 1929 until 1998. The Society of Jesus, through the Jesuit School of Theology in Berkeley, currently staffs the parish.

St. Patrick parishioners are known for their active commitment to the broader West Oakland community. Their important role in the construction of St. Patrick Terrace, a home for the elderly, and of community outreach centers such as Jubilee West and the Prescott-Joseph Center, reflect their generosity and social concern. It remains a vibrant parish and celebrates its multi-ethnic identity as a predominantly African American and Latino community.

ST. JOSEPH BASILICA, ALAMEDA (1885)

Many things have changed, including location, since the first St. Joseph's started serving the spiritual needs of Alameda in 1873. The present church was completed in 1921. One thing that has not changed is that St. Joseph is still serving the spiritual needs of the community. Parish ministries and activities are vibrant and well-attended. The academic needs of the young are being met by St. Joseph Elementary School and St. Joseph Notre Dame High School.

Holy Spirit, Fremont: Father Gerard Moran crowns Rebecca Salazar Queen of 2001 Pentecost Festival

Notre Dame Academy and first St. Joseph's Church, Alameda (photo courtesy of Notre Dame Sisters Archives)

Parish devotions with Father Marco Antonio Figueroa, OFM, pasto[r]

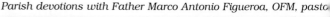

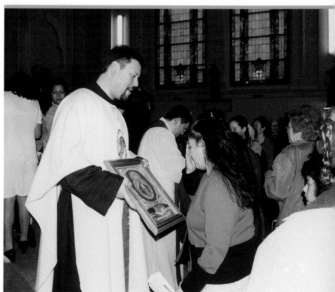

HOLY SPIRIT, FREMONT (1886)

Holy Spirit Parish was established in 1886 to serve the Portuguese community in Centerville (now part of Fremont). In 1919, fire destroyed the church. It was rebuilt in 1926. In 1956 and again in 1969, seating capacity was increased to over 1,000. Fremont is now the fourth largest city in the Bay Area and Holy Spirit has one of the highest weekend Mass attendances in the diocese.

Part of the tradition of Holy Spirit is the annual celebration of the Portuguese Pentecost Festival, the oldest in the State of California. Once a Portuguese tradition honoring Queen Isabel of Portugal, today the Festival has become a multi-ethnic celebration that includes a festival Mass, dinner and dance, the crowning of a Queen, a parade through Fremont and a two day outdoor festival.

ST. ELIZABETH, OAKLAND (1892)

For the last 112 years, the Franciscan Fathers have served the Fruitvale district of Oakland. Throughout their history they have been instrumental in preserving the faith of immigrants from non-English speaking countries. Commissioned by Archbishop Riordan to minister to the German faithful, St. Elizabeth was established as the German National Church within the boundaries of St. Anthony Parish in 1892. Due to the great influx of people displaced by the 1906 San Francisco earthquake, St. Elizabeth was declared a mixed parish. And thus continues to this day. The parish is, however, now heavily Spanish-speaking.

Father Oliver Lynch, pastor from 1961 to 1981, guided the parish through the tumultuous years following Vatican II. He was in the forefront in promulgating the changes almost as soon they were made. He left a great legacy to future Church historians.

Father Paul Vassar (pastor 1981-1994) at St. Columba, Oakland

ST. COLUMBA, OAKLAND (1898)

St. Columba Parish was born in 1898, the child of Sacred Heart, Oakland, and St. Joseph the Worker, Berkeley. The founding pastor was Father Martin Whyte (1898-1900). From its humble beginning in a rented cottage the dream of a complete parish plant would come true with the building of a church, rectory, school, hall and convent. Eventually it would become a partner in Senior Housing.

The original parishioners, about 100 families, were predominantly Irish. After the 1906 earthquake, many Italians moved into the neighborhood, comprising about 35% of the parish.

With the great influx of African Americans during World War II, the parish became very multicultural. Liturgy, which reflects the African American Catholic experience, was initiated during the pastorate of Father Paul Vassar (1981-1994). African American History Month in February draws nationally renowned speakers each year.

ST. AUGUSTINE, PLEASANTON (1901)

In 2000, in an innovative move, St. Augustine parish dedicated a second worship space named St. Elizabeth Ann Seton, also in Pleasanton, and renamed the parish The Catholic Community of Pleasanton. The parish has been at the forefront of many positive developments in the Diocese.
In 2001, the parish celebrated the 100th anniversary of its founding.

ALL SAINTS, HAYWARD (1898)

Established as a mission of St. Leander in 1868, the original church was constructed by parishioners under the direction of Joe Rivers. Made a parish in 1898, a school was opened in1947 under the care of the Dominican Sisters of Adrian, Michigan. The current parish is quite multicultural.

ST. AUGUSTINE, OAKLAND (1907)

St. Augustine Parish was founded in 1907 and served the primarily Irish and Italian Catholic population of North Oakland and South Berkeley. In the first forty-five years of existence, St. Augustine Parish sent many men and women into religious life, including our present Bishop, John S. Cummins, and his late brother, Monsignor Bernard Cummins, whose family was active in the parish and school. Under the leadership of Monsignor Nial McCabe (1951-1969), the parishioners raised funds to build the present church, school and convent, dedicated in 1959. St. Augustine continues to be an ethnically mixed parish of young and older parishioners ministering to the community.

St. Augustine, Oakland: dedication of church

ST. LOUIS BERTRAND, OAKLAND (1908)

St. Louis Bertrand Parish was founded in 1908 with Father James Kiely (1908-1915). Under the leadership of Monsignor John Silva a new church was built in the 1950s. St. Louis Bertrand Parish has grown and been enriched in the last 35 years by its many cultures and ethnicities, with a majority being Latino and African American. Father Edgar Haasl was pastor from 1973 to 1999. The present pastor is Father Stephan Kappler. Dominican Sisters and a permanent deacon serve on the parish staff.

St. Louis Bertrand School was established in 1946, staffed by the Adrian Dominican Sisters. In 1999, the school was combined with St. Cyril School. The campus is located at St. Cyril's.

Parish Festival at St. Louis Bertrand, June 2001

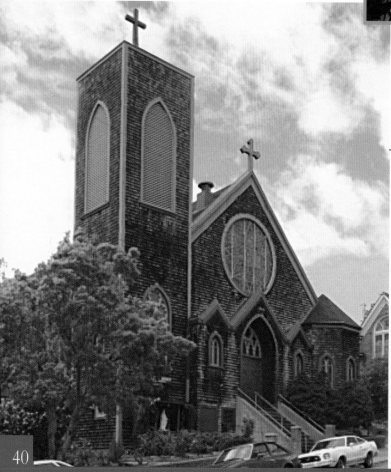

OUR LADY OF MERCY, POINT RICHMOND (1902)

Our Lady of Mercy was established in 1902 to serve the growing population of Santa Fe Railroad and Standard Oil refinery workers and their families in Point Richmond. Father Martin P. Scanlan was appointed the founding pastor, and through his leadership, the church and rectory were constructed and dedicated in 1903.

Our Lady of Mercy was the first Catholic church in Richmond. Originally, the parish territory comprised all of Richmond. Today, the boundaries extend to the immediate Point Richmond area. It is the smallest parish in the diocese.

ST. JARLATH, OAKLAND (1910)

St. Jarlath Parish was founded in 1910. The first Pastor, Father Patrick McHugh, was probably responsible for the name of the parish because he attended St. Jarlath College in County Galway. In 1911 the first church was blessed by Archbishop Riordan and the sermon was preached by the legendary Father Peter C. Yorke. In 1951 a new church was built. The first Mass was celebrated on September 12, 1954 and the church dedicated by Bishop Hugh A. Donohoe, Auxiliary Bishop of San Francisco.

The area of Fruitvale has changed from Irish to ethnically mixed with a large Latino population. Because of this, in the mid-1990's, under the leadership of the pastor, Father Raymond Breton, Mass in Spanish was instituted. The parish school was for many generations staffed by the Sisters of St. Joseph of Carondelet and today remains a vital part of the parish community.

St. Jarlath, Oakland, original altar

ST, AMBROSE, BERKELEY (1909)

The parish was founded in 1909 – the second parish established in Berkeley—as a result of Berkeley's rapid growth, following the earthquake and fire in San Francisco in 1906.

ST. ISIDORE THE FARMER, DANVILLE (1910)

The latest Parish Directory of St. Isidore the Farmer lists 70 parish ministries, running the gamut from Ministry of Consolation to Charismatic Prayer Group to Ministry of Linens and outreach to Latin America. Parish programs include "Little Farmers" which provides church experience for preschoolers, RCIA, Summer Faith Camp, Youth Group, CYO, Bible Study and many others. This is indeed a very, very busy parish. Throughout its history, St. Isidore Parish has grown and prospered and it appears that the trend is continuing.

A Parish
Family Album

ST. LEO THE GREAT, OAKLAND (1911)

In January 1911, the parish of St. Leo the Great was carved from parts of the parishes of Sacred Heart and St. Francis de Sales to serve the newly incorporated city of Piedmont and the Piedmont Avenue neighborhood of Oakland. The founding pastor, Father Owen Lacey (1911 to 1951), oversaw the building of two churches, a school, a rectory and a convent to serve the needs of the predominantly Irish and Italian parishioners. The last fifty years have seen a significant shift in the ethnic mix, demographics and number of people served by this parish. The church continues, as a Piedmont Avenue landmark, to draw and to serve a smaller, vibrant, diverse community of the faithful.

Christmas eve liturgy, 1993, with Father Tim Johnson, pastor

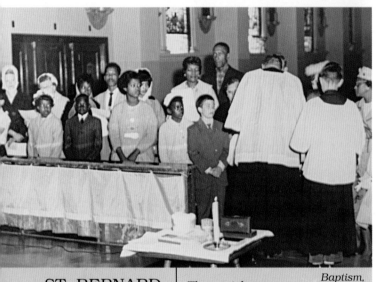

Baptism, 1964

ST. ROSE OF LIMA, CROCKETT (1912)

Since becoming a parish in 1912, St. Rose of Lima has been cared for by the Dominicans for 11 years, diocesan priests for 32 years and the last 46 by the Oblates of Mary Immaculate.

On Christmas Day 1892, with a board resting across two barrels serving as an altar, the first Mass was celebrated in St. Rose Church. Eight months later the church was formally dedicated. The growth of the area necessitated a larger church. C. & H. Sugar donated land and around 1910 the church was moved to the donated land. In 1912 it was established as a parish.

The Oblates took over the administration of the parish in 1955. Eight years later the church burned down and a new and spacious plant was built that today stands as a monument to the faith and generosity of the parishioners and to the leadership of the Oblate Fathers.

ST. BERNARD, OAKLAND (1912)

The parish was established in 1912. Over the years, the church buildings and the community have experienced much change. Originally a Portuguese community, the demographics changed in the 1950s and 1960s, with the parish becoming more and more African American. In the 1980s and 1990s there was a large influx of Spanish-speaking people. It is now about 80% Spanish-speaking but the community is still very much an international one and hosts the local Tongan community.

In 1930 the parish school was established, staffed by the Sisters of the Holy Cross. The school is now administered by laity. Since 1979 the Divine Word Missionaries have been in charge of St. Bernard's and the staff reflects the international character of the parish.

ST. PATRICK, PORT COSTA
(Mission of Crockett)

Port Costa in the late 1800s was a boisterous place along the Straits when the Dominican Fathers from Benicia began to conduct services for the many Catholics living in Post Costa. Without a church, Mass was celebrated wherever space could be found, including the dining room of a boarding house. George McNear donated land and the first St. Patrick Church was dedicated in 1884. This church either burned or blew down and a new church was dedicated in 1898. Thus began the next 100 years of service to the Catholic community.

ST. MARK, RICHMOND
(1912)

From its humble beginnings as a mission church above a grocery store to the present parish plant, St. Mark, as it has done for the last century, continues to serve the Richmond area and to meet new challenges and to offer expanded services to its people. Its community heritage supplies the warmth of understanding and friendship to all who are identified with this parish.

A 1961 parish booklet stated: "History tells us that, It is in the Present, that we look back on the Past, to determine the Future. If this is true, then the future for St. Mark Parish is already determined, based on its glorious Past, and its progressive Catholic Present."

CORPUS CHRISTI, FREMONT
(Niles) (1914)

Established as a mission in 1892 on land donated by the Southern Pacific, it was made a parish in 1914. Initially an agricultural community, the parish now serves a large Latino and Filipino community,

THE DIOCESE OF OAKLAND IS BORN

The Archdiocese, which consisted of the thirteen Bay Area counties, had three new dioceses split off from it at the same time –Santa Rosa, Stockton and Oakland with Oakland to consist of Alameda and Contra Costa Counties. The other dioceses had bishops native to San Francisco appointed-- Bishop Leo T. Maher to Santa Rosa and Bishop Hugh A. Donohoe to Stockton, but Oakland had an unknown prelate from Cleveland appointed to serve as its first bishop, Floyd Lawrence Begin. Begin proved to be an apt choice.

Bishop Begin

Floyd Lawrence Begin was born on February 5, 1902 in Cleveland, Ohio, to Peter Hermengild Begin and Stella McFarland Begin, the eldest of seven children (though three of his siblings died in infancy). Floyd was schooled in Cleveland, where he graduated in 1920 from Cathedral Latin school as class valedictorian. In the same year he entered the Cleveland diocesan seminary, St. John's College, to study for the priesthood. Two years later, he was sent to study in Rome where he completed his studies at the North

On January 13, 1962, the Diocese of Oakland was created, born of the historic Archdiocese of San Francisco.

Bishop Floyd L. Begin

American College and the Propaganda College. On July 31, 1927 he was ordained to the priesthood in Rome by Bishop Ignatius Dubrowski. Following ordination, he pursued advanced studies in canon law, receiving his doctorate from the Apollinaris College in Rome in 1930. He returned to Cleveland, where he was appointed vice-chancellor and secretary to Bishop Joseph Schrembs. He lived and served as chaplain at the Rosemary Johnson Home for crippled children. In 1934, he was named a papal chamberlain, and in 1936, a domestic prelate. Begin served in various capacities until he was named auxiliary Bishop of Cleveland on March 22, 1947. He was ordained bishop on May 1 at St. Agnes Church in Cleveland by Cleveland Bishop Edward F. Hoban. Besides serving as auxiliary Bishop, from 1949 to 1962 Begin served as pastor of the inner-city parish of St. Agnes in Cleveland.

On February 21, 1962, Begin was named the first Bishop of the new Diocese of Oakland. On April 28 he was installed at St. Francis de Sales Cathedral in Oakland by Apostolic Delegate, the Most Reverend Egidio Vagnozzi.

Begin was enthusiastic about coming to Oakland, though legend has it that when he was told that he had been appointed Bishop of Oakland, he responded, "Great! Where's Oakland?" Over the next fifteen years, Begin's enthusiasm, warmth and smile became equally legendary. Typical of this, prior to coming to Oakland, he had photographs of all the priests in Oakland sent to him so he could learn their names before he arrived in Oakland. This gracious gesture reflected Begin's profound desire to love and serve the People of God in Oakland. And this love was amply returned. One pastor recalled that once when Begin visited his parish, the "children swarmed over him as if he were Santa Claus reincarnated. Maybe he was."

Though personally conservative, Begin was not a rigid ideologue. He was perhaps best described by his second Chancellor, Father Brian Joyce, as having a "canonical mind with a pastoral heart." Though trained in canon law, Begin was a good listener with an open mind and open heart, who was not afraid to change his mind when shown good reason. Another priest remembers that Begin was big enough to say, "You're right, I'm wrong" and "I'm sorry." Equally important, he was an able delegator, who trusted the men he placed in charge of an agency or apostolate. Nor did he appoint only "yes, men" to important positions within the diocese. He appointed a mixed cabinet, consisting of young and old, liberal and conservative, showing particular trust in the younger clergy of the diocese. He appointed a series of priests in their early thirties to key positions, including John Cummins, Chancellor; Frank Maurovich, editor of the diocesan newspaper, *The Catholic Voice*; Joseph Skillin, his personal secretary; and Michael Lucid, director of CCD. Balancing the youth were several older, more conservative priests including Monsignors Nicholas Connolly, his Vicar General; John

Bishop Begin arrives via helicopter, 1962

A favorite joke of the era

A HISTORY OF THE DIOCESE OF
OAKLAND

Connolly, Officialis, who became his chief financial officer; Pearse Donovan, superintendent of Catholic Schools; and John McCracken, director of Catholic Charities. He listened to all of them. Begin's style, according to one young priest, "created an atmosphere of openness and forward movement" in the diocese.

Finally, Begin was, again according to Joyce, an incurable "enthusiast for the Church" and an optimist. In one memorable speech, during the midst of the trials of the 1960s, Begin told his priests, "I don't believe things are as bad as they really are."

The Early Years

The evening following Begin's installation a gala banquet was held at the Kaiser Center in Oakland with former Senator and editor of the *Oakland Tribune* William F. Knowland serving as Master of Ceremonies. The mayor of Oakland plus other civic dignitaries from Alameda and Contra Costa counties attended. The following day, the *Tribune* featured a front page color photo of the Bishop. Begin's initial remarks set the tone for his episcopacy. He told the assembled gathering there would "be no second class citizens in the Diocese of Oakland." Earlier in the day he had remarked, "We have come to win Alameda and Contra Costa Counties for Christ. And we have come to do this, not by fire and sword, but by the spreading of Divine Love."

The spreading of Divine Love took on four major dimensions in the first years of Begin's administration—evangelization, vocation, stewardship, and education. In 1963, Begin initiated a "Spiritual Crusade" in which he instructed his priests to go door to door to meet their parishioners, thereby deepening the relationship of priest and people. Placed under the direction of Father Nial McCabe, the *Voice*

recorded that the program reaped a rich spiritual reward.

Begin also sought to increase vocations to the priesthood. In 1963, rather than having one large ordination ceremony at the Cathedral, Begin scheduled ordinations for successive weeks, each week he ordained a new priest in that priest's home parish, a policy that lasted until 1971. The ordination of Father E. Donald Osuna at St. Louis Bertrand was televised by Channel 2. In 1966, the diocese, in conjunction with the Serra Clubs of the diocese, sponsored a massive Vocation Fair at the Oakland Municipal Auditorium—more than 5,000 attended. The Fair was the "first of its kind in the United States," according to historian Peter T. Conmy.

Begin also initiated an innovative stewardship program. He was a firm advocate of "tithing" (returning the first tenth of your income to the Lord) and quickly initiated a "Dignified Giving" program under the direction of Father Thomas Gallagher. His notion was to rid the local Church of such unseemly fundraisers as Bingo and gambling. Begin affirmed in 1964, "I here and now declare the tithing program to be the only norm of Church and charity fundraising in the Diocese of Oakland." The St. Barnabas parish bulletin followed suit, "There will be no more Fiestas, or money making affairs, and tickets sold in the front of church. You can give your offering in a dignified manner by offering your tithe to God." Begin was so passionate about the topic that his only intervention at the Second Vatican Council was about tithing. He also served as Chair of the US Bishops Committee on tithing.

The finances of the diocese were always on a sound footing under Begin, largely due to the ministrations of his chief financial officer, Monsignor John P. Connolly. The diocese received a fair endowment from the Archdiocese at the time of the split, but Connolly insured that the diocese remained financially stable. Connolly was particularly adept at purchasing real estate. He once recalled, "We were buying property all over the two counties. We made marvelous buys and made money on everything. Buy twenty acres always, use ten, sell off the other twenty years later."

Sound financing made possible a rapid expansion of educational facilities. During Begin's first five years, ten elementary schools and three high schools (Moreau in Hayward, under the direction of the Brothers of the Holy Cross; De La Salle in Concord, under the direction of the Christian Brothers; and Carondelet, under the Sisters of St. Joseph of Carondelet) were constructed and opened. Instrumental in their construction, and in creating a professional Building Committee for the diocese was Clem Finney, who oversaw diocesan construction until the 1990s.

The Second Vatican Council

On October 11, 1962, five months after Bishop Begin's installation, Pope John XXIII opened the Second Vatican Council in Rome. In the Pope's opening address, he called for an "*aggiornamento*," quite literally an "updating" of the Church in order to reinvigorate the Gospel truth of "Christ...ever resplendent as the center of history and of life." The Pope also projected an immense optimism about the future of the Church, breaking ranks with the "prophets of doom, who are always forecasting disaster..."

The opening of the Council was met with great enthusiasm by the Catholic faithful in the diocese. Few were aware that the Council would shake the very foundations of the Church that existed in the 1950s. A profound change in the Church's understanding of itself was wrought. The ancient doctrine of the Church as the

Carondelet High School ground breaking (1965)

"People of God" was reasserted. The ultimate aim of the Council, according to Father Frank Norris, was to make the Church a better sign of the Risen Christ in the world. What this meant in practice proved to be the source of much controversy.

Bishop Begin was most enthusiastic about the Council and energetic in implementing its decrees. Begin attended every session of the Council, his enthusiasm and attention never flagging. So close was Begin's identification with the Council, that in later years, when a young cleric read a portion of a Council document to him, Begin snapped, "Don't quote those documents to me. I wrote them!"

Ecumenism

Begin was a strong supporter of the ecumenical movement. Even before the Council opened, Begin sponsored an extraordinary dinner the likes of which had never been seen before in Oakland. On September 13, 1962, against the advice of his consultors, Begin hosted a gathering of more than 150 Protestant ministers, Jewish rabbis, and their wives at the Claremont Hotel. Following the dinner, Jewish, Catholic and Protestant speakers addressed the crowd, but the evening belonged to Begin. In his comments Begin stated simply, "I do not really know why I invited you all here this evening. All I want you to know is that I love you." Begin's profession of love set a positive tone for interfaith relationships that paid dividends years later. Many of the invited guests never forgot Begin's graciousness.

Throughout his episcopacy Begin remained open ecumenically. For example, he spoke at Temple Sinai in Oakland at the invitation of Rabbi William Stern; on another occasion he joined with Episcopal bishop C. Kilmer Myers for an ecumenical prayer service at St. Elizabeth's in Oakland. In November 1963, Begin established a

Bishop Begin with Monsignors Nicholas and John Connolly at the Vatican Council

diocesan Ecumenical Commission under the direction of his chancellor, Father John Cummins, one of the earliest such commissions anywhere in the United States. Dialogues with those of the Baptist and Lutheran faith were conducted. Many parishes joined in the effort; the Cathedral parish of St. Francis developed a close relationship with its neighbor, the First Baptist Church. In the late 1960s the Cathedral parish community walked down the block to join First Baptist in worship. Cathedral rector Father Michael Lucid observed, "Brothers and Sisters in Christ, we Catholics traveled one short block to join you in worship today. It only took us four centuries to walk it!" St. John's Parish in El Cerrito was instrumental in the creation of the Greater Richmond Interfaith Program, which ultimately consisted of more than thirty-one different congregations. Many parishes hosted "Living Room Dialogues," in which small group interfaith discussions were held in people's homes. In April, 1967, the Diocesan Ecumenical

Commission issued a set of guidelines for ecumenical efforts in the parish. The same month the Diocese sponsored the Fourth National Workshop on Christian Unity. The keynote address was delivered by noted Protestant theologian Robert McAfee Brown, but once again Bishop Begin rose to the occasion. In his remarks, Begin proclaimed, " A divided Christianity is a scandal to the world." Further, he noted, ecumenism was "not an event, but daily living in fraternity and charity." Through his efforts, according to one priest, Begin "created an ecumenical spirit in the Diocese of Oakland."

Perhaps the greatest ecumenical endeavor of the era was the founding in 1962 of the Graduate Theological Union (GTU) in Berkeley, a consortium of Protestant seminaries. John Dillenberger, a member of the United Church of Christ, and referred to by some as the

GTU founders Father Kevin Wall, OP and John Dillenberger with Bishop Begin and visitor Hans Kung.

"Protestant version of Pope John," had been persuaded to leave Harvard Theological School to head up the new GTU. The first Catholic contact with the GTU was initiated in 1964 by Dominicans Kevin and Antoninus Wall of St. Albert's College in Oakland. Through their efforts St. Albert's was admitted as the first Catholic Theologate in the GTU. Prior to their

admission, however, they needed to receive the approval of Bishop Begin. To this end, they invited Begin to St. Albert's commencement at which Dillenberger had been asked to speak. According to Antoninus Wall, "John gave a fine talk. We then invited Begin to close the event with some words of his own. Begin went on and on about John and this great development of the GTU." After the graduation, Begin asserted, "The Catholic Church has to become part of the GTU." Kevin Wall informed the Bishop of the Dominicans plans and by July 1964, the Dominicans were admitted to the GTU.

The Jesuits moved their theologate to the GTU in 1966, and the Franciscans followed in 1968. By the 1970s many major religious orders had established Houses of Study in Berkeley so their seminarians could attend the GTU. Oakland became the center for the clerical education of religious orders throughout the West, though students for the Diocese remained at St. Patrick's Seminary in Menlo Park.

Years later, Dillenberger claimed that though Begin might be personally conservative, he was "ahead of every bishop in the country on theological education and liturgy."

The New Liturgy

The most evident changes mandated by the Vatican Council were the changes to the liturgy. Heading the list of changes was the switch from Latin to English or to the vernacular as it was called. The priest was now to face the congregation rather than celebrate Mass with his back to the people. A host of other changes large and small were also introduced. In charge of diocesan implementation was Father Gary Tollner, who affirmed Bishop Begin's stance that "the Diocese of Oakland will not 'jump the gun' on liturgical changes." The changes were scheduled to be introduced the first Sunday of Advent 1964. Tollner gave a preview of the

Father Gary Tollner celebrates the first Mass in English at St. Francis de Sales Cathedral, September 1, 1964

The Cathedral

In 1962, St. Francis de Sales had been named the Cathedral parish for the new Diocese. Rather than build a new Cathedral, Begin observed that that was, "A task I shall leave my successor." He decided to remodel the old church, which had been built in 1893. To perform the remodeling he hired the services of Harold Rambusch. Begin's plan was not for a simple cleaning and restoration, but a bold new plan, that drastically altered the old church. With the priest now facing the people, the Bishop found the venerable stained glass windows behind the altar distracting. "The rather colorful windows in the sanctuary impeded the vision of the service, just as the headlights of an oncoming car do." The stained glass windows were covered over by redwood paneling. The interior was white-washed and the exterior painted in a crème color. The altar rail was removed as were all the statues, except for that of Jesus. In sum, the remodeled building followed Vatican II directives and created "an atmosphere conducive to participation, worship, and prayer."

changes at St. Francis de Sales Cathedral on September 1, with implementation to occur in all the parishes, November 29. A poll in October revealed that an overwhelming number of parishioners approved the change from Latin to English, though some lamented the loss of Latin. "The Mass in Latin gave the feeling of 'home' no matter where in the world you were attending." Nonetheless, another poll in April 1967 revealed that people "by and large" were in favor of the new liturgy. Still some longed for the Latin Mass. In 1968, Tollner oversaw a two-month experiment in which the new liturgy was celebrated in Latin at St. Lawrence O'Toole in Oakland. Though the experiment was terminated, the new Latin Mass was being offered at St. Margaret Mary in Oakland by 1972. In 1989, the parish would receive a special indult to celebrate the Tridentine Rite Mass in Latin.

The desire to return to Latin was maintained by a small minority. Another poll in 1972 indicated that more than 60% of the people polled felt the Mass had become more meaningful in the last five years. And what the Diocese of Oakland became known for was not its traditionalists; what the Diocese became known for was the creativity with which it implemented the new liturgy. The first demonstration of this was the renovation of St. Francis de Sales Cathedral, which claimed to be the "first Cathedral in the United States to be completely remodeled according to the liturgical spirit of the Second Vatican Council."

The remodeled Cathedral was blessed on February 4, 1967. Special music was composed and performed by Father E. Donald Osuna. The entrance procession was greeted by Osuna's beautiful rendition of Psalm 83, sung by the Cathedral choir, "O how awesome is this place. This is none other than the house of God." St. Patrick's Seminary Rector, Father Paul Purta, SS, delivered the homily in which he dubbed the Cathedral, "a tribute to a bishop who will leave nothing undone to translate the message of Vatican II to his people." Purta continued, "the Cathedral is also a sign of desire for Christ's presence, the place that saw the burning bush, a holy place, an awesome place, a place of continuing divine presence."

Much was made of the fact that Begin had chosen a less costly approach to creating a new

Cathedral. Across the Bay in San Francisco protests were mounting over the cost of the new Cathedral being built there. This was not lost on *Voice* editor Frank Maurovich who praised Begin, editorializing, "At a fraction of what it would have cost to build a new Cathedral, the Church has been reconditioned and renewed." Several weeks after the blessing Begin sounded a theme reflective of the era; in an address to inner-city pastors Begin affirmed, "I pledge the resources of the diocese to alleviate the problems of the poor, especially those of minority groups." There would be no protests in Oakland over the new cathedral.

The Cathedral Liturgy

Not everyone was enthused about the new St. Francis. Long-time pastor Monsignor Richard "Pinky" O'Donnell, and many older parishioners whose ancestors had served as models "for the saints who once graced the nave," (now covered over in the remodeling), felt betrayed. The Cathedral parish was located in the heart of the inner city, and as described by Father Donald Osuna, it consisted of "the Greyhound Bus depot across the street, the halfway house for convicted felons down the block, and the dismal hotels that shared the adjoining avenue." The parish congregation had been dwindling for years. Out of these depressed circumstances emerged an extraordinary liturgy and congregation that placed the Diocese of Oakland in the national spotlight. [The following is based largely on an unpublished memoir of Rev. E. Donald Osuna].

In late 1967, Father Osuna was appointed by Bishop Begin to "take charge of the Cathedral worship services and create a 'model of Vatican II liturgy'." Osuna quickly engaged the services of John L. McDonnell, a local attorney, who was also a gifted musician to assist him in forming a Cathedral choir and in developing the new liturgy. Nothing happened until the following summer when Monsignor Michael Lucid was appointed the new rector and Father James Keeley joined the staff as well. According to Osuna, the new staff held a meeting to determine the priorities of the parish. With Keeley's urging liturgy emerged as the top priority or as he put it, "As a church our first priority should be to teach our people to pray." The parish committed more than 25% of its resources to upgrading the liturgy, though the parish did not have enough money to purchase a new organ. The result: McDonnell and Osuna developed an "instrument ensemble: strings, brass, piano", and musicians in lieu of an organ. The ensemble performed songs that ranged from classical to pop and created what came to be known as the "Oakland Cathedral Sound," which soon garnered national attention. In May 1971, *Time* magazine observed, "twice each Sunday, the music runs the scale between such unlikely extremes as Gregorian chant and rock. On one recent Sunday, the mixture embraced both Bach's *Air for the G-String* and *Amazing Grace*. On another, included a Hayden trio, Bob Dylan's *The Times, They Are A-Changin'* and Luther's *A Mighty Fortress Is Our God*. Worshipers come from all over the Bay Area." The music also attempted to reflect the ethnic make-up of the parish. Soon

St. Francis de Sales prior to renovation

St. Francis de Sales interior before renovation

Negro spirituals and Spanish hymns were featured regularly.

But the Cathedral liturgy was not merely innovative musically, it also began to employ the visual and dramatic arts. Dance, slide presentations, photography, innovative preaching, all became regular features in the Cathedral liturgies, that were dubbed "creative celebrations." Contemporary art forms were blended with traditional images and rites. In late 1969, the Cathedral featured an Advent series entitled "We Hold a Strange Hope" to explore how to maintain hope in the midst of the social chaos engulfing the United States. The first week featured four blown-up portraits hanging in the sanctuary—Che Guevara, Joan Baez, the Rev. Martin Luther King, Jr. and Neil Armstrong. The following week the portraits were replaced by one large one—Pope John the XXIII. The sermons reflected on the portraits, and in the case of Pope John, the homilist had a dialogue with the late pope, who concluded, "Tell me,…am I the only one who holds a 'strange hope'?"

As news of the Cathedral liturgy spread, the congregation began to grow beyond local parishioners; people from throughout the diocese began flocking to the Cathedral. Also attracted were students from neighboring colleges as well as professors. On any Sunday the congregation might include noted liturgists, distinguished scripture scholars, theologians, visiting bishops

Cathedral after renovation

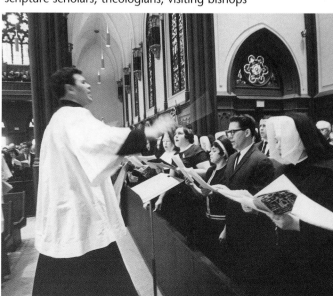

Father Donald Osuna with Cathedral Choir at Dedication

Bishop Begin became an outspoken supporter of the Rumford Act and opponent of Proposition 14. Begin's background in Cleveland had well-prepared him for this sort of advocacy. He had served as pastor of St. Agnes parish, an increasingly African American parish, and he had witnessed the discrimination against his people there. He had earned some fame for working to integrate the Knights of Columbus in that diocese. He spoke forthrightly on racial issues. He told the Serra Club in Cleveland, "Christ did not become man to save only the whites," and more controversially, "Adam and Eve were black." He brought his forthrightness with him to Oakland, and he quickly joined the fair housing fray.

On June 21, 1963 his newspaper, *The Catholic Voice*, endorsed the Rumford Act while it was still being debated in the state legislature, though the editorial condemned the use of confrontational protests such as those being sponsored by CORE in Sacramento. The following week, however, Begin endorsed the right of minorities to engage in non-violent demonstrations and prodded federal and state legislators to act on fair housing. In August, the bishop sent a memo to all his priests ordering them to preach "a solid sermon on the subject of racial justice based on the truths of faith and true Americanism."

Institutional supports began to develop as well. In late spring, 1963, the Diocese's first Catholic Interracial Council (CIC) was formed in Berkeley under the leadership of Thomas McGowan, a contract specialist for the federal government, and C. Herbert Clemens, a graduate student at Cal, and at the inspiration of Dr. Raymond Sontag, a professor of history at the University of California at Berkeley. Another branch was soon established in Oakland, with Father William O'Donnell assigned as chaplain. (Thus began the storied career of the diocese's most ardent champion of social justice).

Free Speech Movement at University of California at Berkeley, 1964; Joan Baez singing

The early CIC addressed a number of key issues such as education, unemployment, parish and community relations, and of course, housing. In January 1963 the Diocese sent representatives, including Chancellor Monsignor John Cummins to the National Conference of Religion and Race in Chicago, which featured Dr. Martin Luther King, Jr. Within the year an ecumenical East Bay Conference on Religion and Race had been established with Cummins serving as vice-chairman.

One of the leading and most passionate Catholic laymen on civil rights was Dr. Raymond Sontag, who was instrumental in the foundation of the diocese's CIC. He delivered many public addresses challenging his fellow Catholics to confront the issue of race. For Begin and Cummins, Sontag represented the conscience of the Diocese.

The central battle remained fair housing. In December, as CREA circulated petitions to place its initiative on the ballot, *The Voice* advised, "We strongly urge you not to sign such a petition." Its advice went unheeded and Proposition 14 was placed on the ballot. Begin continued to oppose the initiative. The front page headline of *The Voice* March 6, 1964 read, "BISHOP BEGIN BACKS RUMFORD ACT—Opposes State Initiative." The CICs joined Begin in agitating against the bill. In April, Rumford himself spoke at several meetings of the Berkeley and Oakland CICs. At one meeting Father O'Donnell articulated what was a common belief of the era, claiming civil rights to be "the greatest moral and social problem of our age." The CIC developed a group of speakers who traveled throughout the diocese, speaking against the proposition. They also began a voter registration drive, registering more than 1,000 new voters by July. Then on June 28, Bishop Begin ordered that a letter from him, opposing Proposition 14, be

read at all the churches in the diocese. The letter, written by Chancellor Cummins, but signed and issued by Begin without hesitation, read in part, "We are...firm in our judgment that the initiative measure proposed as Proposition 14 next fall is of such a nature as to contradict what is clear and universal Catholic teaching on the rights and duties of those who own property. Proposition 14 is a moral issue insofar as it concedes absolute rights to property owners with no reference to the rights of others. In the interest of justice and charity it should be defeated." Begin's opposition was the most forthright of any bishop in California, and established him as a moral leader in the civil rights struggle.

Unfortunately, Begin's efforts and those of the CIC were not enough. Proposition 14 passed by an overwhelming two to one majority. Speaking for the Bishop, Cummins lamented, "We regret the judgment on Proposition 14. We hope it will not be an occasion to promote injustice." Begin, who was away at the Vatican Council, spoke of his disappointment and "personal embarrass-ment" at the passage of Prop. 14. Father Ralph Brennan was equally blunt in his assessment. He opined, "The general Catholic population was very unaware of what social justice meant."

Despite the setback, the CIC continued its efforts to ensure fair housing. In 1966, the proposition would be declared unconstitutional by the California Supreme Court, a judgment that was affirmed by the US Supreme Court the following year. Begin hailed the courts' decisions.

Many Catholics redoubled their efforts in the fight for racial justice. Several individuals traveled to Mississippi to work as Freedom workers in 1965, while other journeyed to the famed March on Selma the same year. Countless others participated in many local protests, working with the CIC and East Bay Conference on Religion and Race. Many priests and women religious found themselves in public protests for the first time, though the sight became more familiar as the decade progressed. The CIC did enjoy one local victory as the Diocese approved a resolution that required all companies doing business with the diocese to adhere to the diocese's non-discrimination policy in hiring.

United Farmworkers (UFW)

While Begin was a strong advocate in the cause of civil rights, he was not as strong in his advocacy of the rights of farmworkers. Nonetheless, tremendous numbers within the diocese acted in support of Cesar Chavez and his movement. Cesar Chavez and Dolores Huerta established the National Farm Workers Association (NFWA) in 1962 (the NFWA later became the United Farm Workers (UFW) in 1966); in 1965 they joined the Filipino-led Agricultural Workers Organizing Committee in a strike against grape growers beginning at

Delano. The strike would become the longest agricultural strike in the state's history. The Farmworkers' movement had a distinctly Catholic air to it—the majority of migrant workers were Mexicans and Filipinos. Catholic symbols such as the image of our Lady of Guadalupe were prominently displayed at rallies and marches, and Mass and prayer meetings played an integral role in organizing efforts.

The reception of the NFWA in the diocese was largely positive. As the 1965 Delano strike unfolded, *The Voice*, under the editorship of Father Frank Maurovich, ran a series of articles most sympathetic to the strikers. In November, a Maurovich editorial urged growers to recognize the farmworkers union, and stressed the need to respect "the dignity of the human person." A March 17, 1966 front page headline asserted, "BISHOPS BACK FARMWORKERS." Several from the diocese joined Chavez's famous pilgrimage

Civil Rights demonstration at Oakland City Hall; Chancellor John Cummins leads the prayer, 1965

Father William O'Donnell at UFW protest, late 1960s

Father Antonio Valdivia at UFW protest in front of Safeway

march from Delano to Sacramento, including Clem and Reggie Finney and family.

From 1965 through 1975, groups within the diocese actively supported the UFW. Parish groups joined protest marches, and picketed Safeway and other stores that carried non-union products. When the UFW called for a grape boycott to bring economic pressure on the growers, residents of the East Bay responded enthusiastically. As one priest noted, "Some young children never tasted a grape until they were five years old." Parishes also supplied material and monetary support, sending numerous "caravans" to Delano. And when organizers came to the city, several parishes provided housing and meeting rooms. St. Elizabeth's allowed UFW organizers to stay in the old parish convent, on which they unfurled a large banner proclaiming, "HUELGA!" (STRIKE!). Chavez was a frequent visitor to Oakland during the decade, speaking to numerous parish groups, and on one occasion speaking from the pulpit at St. Louis Bertrand.

When the lettuce boycott began in 1970, Oakland once again enthusiastically supported Chavez. When some criticized the use of the Mass at farmworker rallies, Fr. Bill O'Donnell answered, "When a rally speaks to the need for truth, nonviolence and justice, it seems that the Mass belongs with that kind of congregation." By this time O'Donnell was actively involved in the farmworker struggle, often putting his body on the line for the cause. In May 1969, he was arrested for the first time at a sit-in at Safeway headquarters; by 2000, O'Donnell was to have been arrested more than 200 times for various causes.

In 1975, the state of California passed the Agricultural Labor Relations Act, guaranteeing the farmworkers the right to organize, and setting up an orderly process for union elections. The result was a respite in the decade-old battle.

The Vietnam War

More divisive than the Farmworkers' struggle was the passion unleashed by the Vietnam War. Not surprisingly, Catholics, like other Americans, were deeply divided over the issue that rent the entire fabric of the American social order. Again, like other Americans, the vast majority of Catholics began the 1960s avidly supporting American intervention and the battle against communism in Vietnam. From the Gulf of Tonkin Resolution in 1964 through the end of the war in 1973 that support would be sorely tested.

Early editorials in *The Catholic Voice* supported the effort to combat communism. However, by 1966 the escalation in bombing and troop deployment began to raise questions. In June of that year a group of Bay Area priests, including

several from Oakland, urged a halt to the bombings in Vietnam. By September, *The Voice* called for an end to escalation and the need for negotiation. By August, 1967 it asked, "Is it time to withdraw?" and encouraged the beginning of a gradual disengagement.

By then, protests were becoming larger and more violent. In October 1967 downtown Oakland was torn apart by the Stop the Draft Week riots. During the riots, a group of clergy including Father George Crespin, waded into the midst of the rioters to act as peacemakers. They were unsuccessful. Other priests, such as St. Mary's College professor Peter Riga, openly encouraged draft card burnings, while others such as George Crespin and Bill O'Donnell provided counseling for young Catholic men who sought conscientious objector status, and

Jesuits from Berkeley protest the Vietnam War, 1971

Franciscan Father Oliver Lynch loads food for Delano strikers

explored the possibility of achieving selective CO status. They supported one such court case that resulted in a landmark court ruling.

By 1968, the country and the diocese were deeply divided over Vietnam. A poll in *The Voice* indicated that 33% of the people in the diocese supported the war effort, 33% opposed it, and 34% wanted a peace conference. The division was also reflected in the heightened rhetoric. One letter to *The Voice* accused the paper of "reading like the *Hanoi Daily Bladder*." In 1970, Riga was banned from preaching at St. Monica's parish in Moraga because, according to pastor Father Edward Casey, "Father Riga's sermons are too political and disturbing to the people."

In 1970, President Nixon's expansion of the war with the bombing of Cambodia ignited a storm of protest. The Oakland seminarians studying at St. Patrick's Seminary issued a proclamation against the war and joined the other seminary students in a "strike"—the "cessation of normal activities" at the seminary. Their statement protested the "immoral and thoroughly unjustified act of escalation and aggression." At the same time, the three Cathedral priests condemned the war as immoral, with rector Monsignor Michael Lucid reading a prepared statement to the 10:30 Mass community. "Our position is that peace in Vietnam is a moral necessity." And, according to the rector, their statement was "surprisingly well received." Bishop Begin's response was more measured. In conjunction with the diocesan Priests' Senate, Begin sent simultaneous cables to President Nixon and to the government of North Vietnam calling for the withdrawal of troops from Cambodia, Laos, and South Vietnam.

Protests continued to mount. Holy Names College and St. Mary's College established "peace centers" on campus. Several parishes such as Mary Help of Christians in Oakland and

Holy Spirit Newman in Berkeley declared themselves "sanctuary parishes," providing protection for young men seeking to avoid the draft and for soldiers and sailors who refused to go to Vietnam.

As divisions increased, the diocese attempted to encourage and sustain a more civil discourse. In December 1970, the Diocesan Social Justice Commission, working with Robert Pickus of the World Without War Council as a consultant, issued "Guidelines for Work in the War/Peace Field." The Guidelines were intended to be "constructive" and emphasized that "change in a person's will and a coherent body of thought as to how we are to move toward a world order are essential for ending war." A "peace intern" was hired and "response sessions" were held throughout the diocese. The sessions were not intended to address Vietnam specifically, but were to address the larger question of how to create a more peaceful world. As the diocesan peace intern put it, "We are not peaceniks tearing down," but ordinary people building up.

In a similar vein, Dan and Rose Lucey, one of the leading couples of the Oakland Christian Family Movement, proposed the creation of a National Peace Academy to balance the service academies. In 1984, their dream was finally fulfilled.

But neither the Luceys nor the guidelines could stem the increasing violence and strife surrounding protests against the Vietnam war. Mercifully, the war ended in 1973.

Flatland Fathers

Unfortunately violence was increasing everywhere in the late 1960s.

In the early 1960s, the Diocese had established a formal Commission on Social Justice under the direction of Father John Cummins, and in 1968, it hired a full-time staff person, Sister Miriam Thomas McManus, SNJM. Besides war, the Commission forthrightly addressed the issue of racism and violence, encouraging sermons to be preached on these issues. During the previous summer, known as the "long hot summer", race riots had ripped through several US cities, most violently in Detroit and Newark. The federal government investigated the cause of the riots and issued a "Report on Civil Disorders," which came to be known as the Kerner Report. One conclusion: the United States was moving toward two increasingly separate societies—one black and one white. The Diocese paused to reflect on the Commission's findings. The Adult Education Program under the direction of Father Brian Joyce, sponsored a number of meetings throughout the diocese on "Civil Disorders and Our Community in 1968."

Even with the formal efforts at the diocesan level to work toward social justice, the real work was being done at the parish level. One group that became quite effective, and even legendary, was the Flatland Fathers, an extraordinary group of priests from Oakland's inner-city parishes with "a radical commitment to urban ministry." The group had begun as the East Oakland Clergy in 1967, but soon expanded to include West Oakland clergy as well. The Fathers struggled with a new understanding of priesthood, a priesthood not content to stay in the rectory, but which waded into the community to share their people's experience. And with their people they

Father Clarence Howard at St. Patrick's in Oakland

grappled with the relentless disturbances and dislocations of the 1960s and 70s. This talented collection of priests brought hope and commitment to areas of the city forsaken by many. Included in this group were men like Fathers Ed Haasl of St. Louis Bertrand, John Maxwell of St. Andrew-St. Joseph, James Keeley of St. Benedict, William Kennedy of St. Columba, Ralph Brennan of St. Louis Bertrand, and several other young priests. Grounding the group and providing guidance were "two wise men" who were known for their "wisdom and gentleness"-- Fathers Oliver Lynch, OFM, of St. Elizabeth's and Clarence Howard, SVD, of St. Patrick's, both of whom are considered saints by many.

The Flatland Fathers became deeply involved in community affairs, as their parishes sponsored summer programs for inner-city youth, developed senior and low-cost housing, and other community programs. They attempted to take advantage of federal poverty programs. They strongly supported Cesar Chavez and the UFW struggle and opposed the Vietnam War. Most controversial, the Flatland Fathers openly engaged the Black Panther Party, whose violent

rhetoric and militant style offended many Catholics. The Fathers however, believed the Panthers represented a distinct voice within the community that needed to be heard. In June 1967, Bobby Seale addressed the East Bay Conference on Religion and Race and told them, "The Black Panther Party is an attempt to put Black Power into a form that can be flexed. We live in a racist society, so we have to defend ourselves against unemployment, bad education, and racist cops." In May 1968, several of the Fathers joined an ecumenical coalition that urged the Mayor of Oakland and the Chief of Police "to deal [openly]with the Black Panther Party." In 1973, the Fathers took out a full page ad in the *Oakland Tribune* in support of Bobby Seale's candidacy for Mayor. The same ad had been declined by *The Catholic Voice*.

The Right to Life

Though Begin admired the commitment of the Flatland Fathers, their activities made him quite nervous. As the 1960s wore on, Begin became less enthusiastic about public protests, as protests escalated and seemed to become direct

Right to Life protest at abortion clinic

attacks against the institutions of authority such as the state, the police, and even the Church. Speaking in the language of his era, Begin warned, "Vilification of the police is a communist tactic."

One protest Bishop Begin did enthusiastically support was the fight against the liberalization of abortion laws. As early as May 1963 *The Catholic Voice* warned of the coming battle in the California state legislature, urging readers to write letters to oppose the "Therapeutic Abortion Act," which proposed to allow women to have abortions with the consent of their doctors for medical reasons. As the proposed bill made its way through the legislature, *The Voice* ran periodic editorials against it. In 1965 it opined, "The law must shout even louder in behalf of the unborn, for he has no voice to speak for himself." By December 1966 Begin stepped up the attack on the bill. He sent out more than 80,000 letters to people in the diocese, urging them to oppose the bill. Despite these efforts the bill became law in June 1967. Bishop Begin was appalled. *The Voice* featured Begin's denunciation of the Bill on the front page, "The death of the innocent and an immoral, willful taking of life has the sanction of legislation in the state of California." Begin vowed to fight. In a controversial move, Begin wrote personal letters to the legislators in Alameda and Contra Costa Counties who voted for the bill, asking them to explain their vote. His action was condemned by the *San Francisco Chronicle*, which ran an editorial entitled, "Bishop Begin's Political Quiz," arguing that he had violated the separation of Church and state. But *The Voice* countered that abortion was a "moral" not a "political" issue, and therefore the bishop had to speak out. Begin did.

Though no organized Catholic response developed, many Catholics became involved in the Northern California Right to Life Association. Begin openly voiced his support for a group of

protesters known as "Voice of the Unborn," and he declared December 28, 1971, the Feast of the Holy Innocents, a "day of reparation for the crime of abortion." That same year, an emergency pregnancy counseling service, Birthright, was established in Oakland. Founded in Toronto in 1968, Birthright would have ten chapters operating in the Bay Area by 1973.

Then on January 22, 1973, a day dubbed by Bishop Begin as "the worst day in our history," the U.S. Supreme Court in its *Roe v. Wade* decision, virtually approved "abortion on demand." Begin asserted, "I call upon all right thinking Americans to do anything and everything to reverse this decision." Many Catholics took to the streets in protest at abortion clinics and at hospitals that provided abortions. Begin came out in support of a constitutional amendment, guaranteeing the right to life. The Diocesan Council of Catholic Women began a petition drive. The following year on January 22, Begin ordered every church in the diocese to celebrate a Mass of reparation at 7p.m. Begin also issued a pastoral letter, "Affirming Human Life."

About the same time, a Diocesan Pro-Life Committee was formed under the leadership of Sister Leonard Donovan, SHF, assistant director of adult education for the Diocese. The committee's role was largely educative, and they sponsored workshops and talks. They encouraged each parish to develop a pro-life committee. In 1977, they traveled to Sacramento to participate in a Rally for Life, and in future years busses were chartered for the journey to Sacramento to support demonstrations for the Human Life Amendment.

During the 1980s the right to life movement became more combative, utilizing the protest techniques learned in the civil rights struggles of the 1960s. In 1981, a sit-in was held at Planned

Parenthood and abortion clinics in Walnut Creek. In 1985, Father Terry Tompkins of St. John Vianney was arrested and sent to jail for protests in Concord. In 1987, Operation Rescue came to Concord and further arrests ensued.

Less confrontational tactics were also pursued. In 1984, Sister Maureen Webb, SNJM, professor of Bioethics at Holy Names College, joined the Respect Life Office. Together with Sister Donovan, she felt that a more positive "pro-active" approach was necessary. Together they established a home for "women in distress," to provide women an alternative to abortions. (The Diocese had sponsored an earlier effort known as Mary Crest, but it had closed in 1970). With the assistance of the St. Vincent de Paul Society's Olga Morris, the Casa Vincentia was opened. The Casa ultimately occupied the convent at St. Cyril's Church in Oakland, and began providing a much needed service.

Other positive developments included the Respect Life Office's post-abortion ministry known as "Shalom," begun in 1990, and later renamed "After the Choice." Both programs sought to assist the healing of women suffering from post-abortion trauma. In 1994, nine pro-life groups began gathering for prayer breakfasts at St. Isidore in Danville. And in 1996, St. Barnabas in Alameda began to offer twenty-four hour Eucharistic adoration to end the "assault on life, especially abortion."

As of 2002, the Respect Life Commission continues to work to end the scourge of abortion, and to promote a Culture of Life in opposition to the widespread culture of death.

Office of Criminal Justice

In 1975, Bishop Begin was deeply affected by a visit to Santa Rita jail in Pleasanton. In response he issued a pastoral letter "On Criminal Justice and Corrections," in which he asserted "the vindictive attitude of 'lock them up and throw away the key' is not consistent with human dignity and cannot be tolerated of any Christian." Begin called for a comprehensive program of real rehabilitation for the inmates. He established a new chancery office, the Office of Criminal Justice, which he placed under the direction of Frank Buismato, OFM. By the 1990s, the office had been placed under the auspices of

Bus to Sacramento for Human Life Amendment Rally

Catholic Charities, with Deacon Frank Beville program coordinator.

TURMOIL WITHIN THE CHURCH

By the early 1970s, the endless social traumas of the past decade had taken an enormous toll. Catholics found themselves deeply divided over issues such as the Vietnam War, civil rights, and other social issues. More distressing, however, was the sense that the Church was in serious crisis: Mass attendance was down, Catholic schools were declining, men and women were leaving religious life in droves, traditional devotions had all but disappeared, and internal divisions racked the Church. Bishop Begin noted "We have not escaped the malaise that has affected the Church throughout the United States." Some blamed the malaise on the changes initiated by the Vatican Council, especially the liturgical changes. Others argued the Church had become too political. For some change had come too quickly; for others it had not come fast enough. Whatever the cause, deep divisions beset the church.

Some pointed to the controversial encyclical *Humanae Vitae* issued by Pope Paul VI in 1968, which reiterated the Church's traditional teaching banning the use of artificial birth control. Its publication met with widespread dissent, an unusual reaction to a papal encyclical. Though Begin urged that the encyclical "be accepted and obeyed," *The Catholic Voice* published comments by a noted local scholar, who predicted the decision would eventually be overturned. *The Voice* editorial counseled, "While the individual conscience is the last word, it cannot ignore such authoritative pronouncements." Unfortunately, many Catholics did just that—they either resisted or ignored the encyclical. Opposition to the encyclical severely eroded Church authority as people who had never defied a papal directive now found themselves doing so.

Equally distressing to many Catholics was the departure of so many priests and Sisters from the religious life. The Council and the era caused many to reevaluate their vocations, and many decided they could best serve God elsewhere. Bishop Begin took these departures quite hard. According to Margaret Mealey, long time executive secretary of the National Council of Catholic Women, Begin was "heartsick" over the departures. But no departure hurt him more than that of Monsignor Joseph Skillin, whom he regarded as a son. For nine years, Skillin had served as Begin's secretary, and in 1971 Skillin had received the prestigious appointment as rector of the Cathedral. Then in 1973, Skillin abruptly left the priesthood to get married. The wedding was front page news in the *Oakland Tribune*. Skillin's departure left Begin hurt and shocked. To make matters worse, the marriage had been performed by Skillin's Cathedral associate, Father Donald Osuna. Begin suspended Osuna, leaving the Cathedral community reeling. In typical Begin fashion, his "pastoral heart" overcame his "canonical mind" and he dramatically reinstated Osuna three months later at the Cathedral at Midnight Mass on Christmas Eve, 1973. At Bishop Begin's invitation, Osuna joined the Bishop to concelebrate the Mass. When he entered the church, the faithful erupted with a standing ovation which according to one observer, "nearly brought the roof down." More surprisingly, in 1975, Osuna was appointed rector of the Cathedral, despite the protests of many senior clergy. As always, Begin did what he thought was best for the Church in Oakland. Again in typical fashion, before his death, Begin even reconciled with Skillin.

Nonetheless, the departure of his priests grieved Begin, as it did many Catholics.

THE END OF THE BEGINNING

Catholic Charities

The men and women of diocesan Catholic Charities are some of the unsung heroes of the history of the diocese. Daily, often unnoticed, they bring sustenance and assistance to the needy and disadvantaged of the diocese.

The Archdiocese of San Francisco had established an Alameda County branch of Archdiocesan Catholic Charities under the direction of Father Joseph Mulkern in 1934. Though his title was assistant director of Catholic Charities, for all intents and purposes he was Oakland's first director. He was succeeded by Father Charles Hackel in 1944. When the Diocese was created in 1962, the new Diocesan office of Catholic Charities came under the direction of Monsignor John T. McCracken, who served until 1972, succeeded by Father William Macchi.

Catholic Charities oversaw a wide variety of charities including family counseling, child care, senior services, senior housing, hospitals and deaf work. Over the years it developed employment services, prison ministry, refugee resettlement, work with the handicapped, alcohol rehabilitation, and other endeavors. The many

Bishop Begin directed the Diocese through an extraordinarily turbulent time, but it was not all turmoil.

The first fifteen years of the Diocese's history witnessed many less contentious achievements as well.

efforts of the diocesan Catholic Charities would require a separate book; suffice it to say they have made a substantial contribution to the well-being of the diocese.

Special Religious Education

One of the most innovative programs initiated in the diocese was a program to provide religious education for the "developmentally disabled" or the "mentally handicapped" as they were then called. In 1966, Sister M. Fidelia, SSJ, operating under the auspices of CCD and Catholic Social Services, began the program. The following year a Catholic Committee for the Retarded was established. Parishes were encouraged to establish centers to assist the developmentally disabled. By 1968, some twenty-seven parishes had centers. In March of that year, Bishop Begin confirmed a special religious education class. Rather than preach a sermon, Begin noted, "I let them preach to me." Regular special Masses were celebrated annually.

In 1974, Concord House, the first residence for adults with developmental disabilities, was established under the auspices of Catholic Charities.

By the mid-1970s the Special Religious Education program had hit a lull, so Sister Aurora Perez, SHF, was brought in, in Fall 1976, to energize the program. In 1978, she studied for her Masters degree in special religious education at the University of Loyola at Chicago. Since her return in 1979, the SPRED program (Special Religious Education for the Developmentally Disabled) has grown and flourished. By 2001, there were 25 SPRED centers, including three for the Spanish-speaking, and more than 400 participants in the diocese. The SPRED program employs a large number of dedicated volunteers and catechists, as each student or "friend" as they are called, is given special one-on-one attention. To date the program has been enormously successful.

The Saint Vincent De Paul Society

The most important charitable organization run by the laity is the St. Vincent de Paul Society, which operates under the umbrella of Diocesan Catholic Charities. The Society was founded in France in 1833 by Frederic Ozanam to provide the spiritual and corporal works of mercy. It was brought to the United States in 1845. The first conference, as the parish societies are called, in Oakland was established in 1878 at Sacred Heart. However, by 1892 the first foundation had dissolved. It was not until 1931, during the height of the Great Depression, that the Society was re-established at St. Mary's parish in Oakland. From there it spread rapidly throughout the diocese. The parish conference remains the basic means of getting food and assistance to the needy in the diocese.

In 1962, the Society purchased land in East Oakland to create a central headquarters or "Center" as it was called. The new facility was opened and blessed in March 1964 and included offices, a large warehouse, workshops, repair shop, and a thrift store. By 1987, nine thrift stores were in operation throughout the diocese.

Catholic Charities assists immigrant families

SPRED Liturgy

In 1976, the Society broke ground for the St. Vincent de Paul Dining Room in downtown Oakland at 23rd Street and San Pablo. Though funded by the Society, the free dining facility was to be run by the Congregation of the Little Brothers of the Good Shepherd, whom the Society brought from Albuquerque, New Mexico. The Society's effort received a major boost when Bishop Begin wrote them a check for $25,000, an act he repeated when the Dining Room was dedicated on September 12, 1976. The first meal was served on September 20, 1976, and by the end of the month 2,279 free meals had been served. By 1981, more than 11,000 meals were being served each month, a number that jumped to 32,000 by the mid-1980s. In 1986, the Daughters of Charity replaced the Little Brothers. Whoever has been in charge, the dining room has depended on the countless number of volunteers who have cooked and served meals at the dining room.

St. Vincent de Paul truck

Groundbreaking at St. Vincent de Paul Dining Room, Oakland; (from left) Oakland Mayor John Reading, Building Committee Chairman Mike Hester with shovel, Good Shepherd Brother Victor Nolan, Bishop Floyd Begin, and Cy Gilfether, St. Vincent de Paul president.

An early female counterpart to the St. Vincent de Paul Society was the Catholic Ladies Aid Society that was begun at St. Mary's parish in Oakland in 1887 by Father Michael King. The Society provided direct material relief to the poor. Personal service to the poor was stressed; acts of "hidden charity" were pursued such as the collection and distribution of food and clothing.

The San Antonio Youth Project

One of the diocese's more innovative endeavors was the San Antonio Youth Project begun at St. Anthony's parish by William "Bill" Parr. In 1962, Parr taught religion at St. Anthony's school, as well as Saturday Confirmation class. He became aware of the growing problem of adolescent boys who were having serious difficulties at home and school. He began a Saturday "work and recreation program." In 1967, he rented a fourplex on East 15th St. and began caring for about twenty boys. In 1973, a larger facility was purchased on 11th Avenue. Many of the boys Parr worked with were referred by the California Youth Authority or the Alameda County Juvenile Court. Parr provided extraordinary service to the young men of east Oakland.

There are many other developments too vast to recount here such as the efforts of the Family Life Office, or of the Catholic Youth Organization, or the Catholic Worker houses. These and many other agencies have made significant contributions to the history of the diocese.

Catholic Schools:
A Time of Challenge

During the 1970s, the construction of new Catholic schools slowed considerably. In fact, enrollment in elementary schools had begun to decline, and several schools were closed by 1973. A profound shift was occurring in the staffing of the schools, as many communities of women religious began to withdraw from the schools. By 1971, the number of lay school teachers surpassed the number of school Sisters for the first time in the diocese's history. With the increase of lay employees, came a dramatic increase in school budgets. And with increased

St. Vincent de Paul Dining Room, 1977

budgets came increased tuition. Despite these changes Catholic schools remained strong and continued to provide the diocese with excellent service.

The inner-city schools were particularly hard hit during the 1960s, though the diocese maintained its strong commitment to inner-city schools. Instrumental in this regard was a group of extraordinary women religious who served as principals and kept these schools thriving. Bishop Cummins refers to these women as the "Magnificent Seven:" Sister Sebastian Adza of St. Bernard's, Sister Rose Marie Hennessy of St. Elizabeth's, Sister Eugene Francis at St. Patrick's, Sister Miriam Thomas McManus at St. Mary's, Sister Diana Pellegrino at St. Louis Bertrand, Sister Celestine O'Brien at St. Francis de Sales, and Sister Patricia Kinney at St. Anthony's.

In 1978, Sr. Sebastian Adza initiated a major diocesan fundraising effort to provide tuition assistance to needy families. The program dubbed FACE (Family Aid—Catholic Education)

has provided thousands of dollars of grants and assisted Catholic schools tremendously. Instrumental in the foundation of FACE were Edward and Barbara Morrill (Barbara had served on the first Diocesan school board in 1971), who served as the founding chaircouple.

Through the efforts of FACE, and the efforts of many, many volunteers at the parish and diocesan levels, Catholics schools have remained strong and vibrant. In 1979, the first non-clerical superintendent was appointed, Sister Rose Marie Hennessy, OP, who served until 1994, when she was replaced by the first lay superintendent, Dr. Ann Manchester.

The Death of Bishop Begin

On February 5, 1977, Bishop Begin celebrated his 75th birthday, and submitted his resignation to Rome. A major convocation was planned for May 1 to celebrate his retirement and honor his fifteen years as bishop. Unfortunately, Bishop Begin did not live to see this occasion. In late

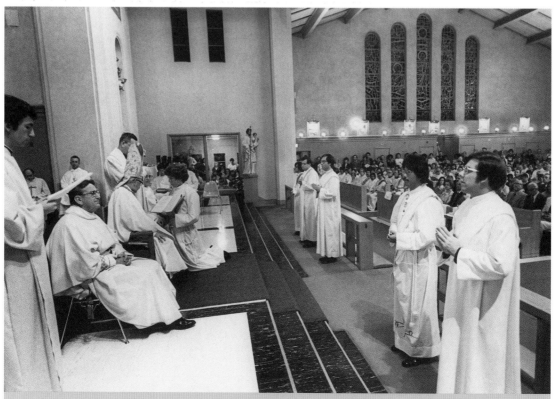

Bishop Begin presides at his last ordination, St. Lawrence O'Toole, 1977

1976, the cancer, which had first been diagnosed in 1972, recurred. By early 1977, Begin was growing weaker by the day, but he struggled to fulfill his duties until his replacement was appointed. As he declined, he was faithfully cared for by Father Jerrold Kennedy and his long-time housekeepers, Sisters Lydia and Thomasine. As death approached, Begin rallied his strength for one last great duty—the ordination of five priests at St. Lawrence O'Toole Church. On April 22, against the advice of his doctors and close advisors, Begin left his sick bed to ordain five seminarians: Michael Galvan, John Fernandes, David McCarthy, Robert Charm, and Fred Riccio. Begin presided magnificently at the ceremony. Sisters Lydia and Thomasine were in awe. They noted that before the ordination he was so weak, that we "prayed he would make it through the ceremony." But as Sister Lydia observed, "When we heard his voice in the church, we felt it must have been a miracle or a special grace he was receiving."

His duty completed, Begin returned to the hospital where he died four days later on April 26, 1977.

Begin had presided over fifteen years of intense change and turmoil with immense grace and good cheer. The *Oakland Tribune* summed up his career simply, "The entire Eastbay was a better place because of his long and productive career." His clergy praised him as "pastoral, accessible, flexible, fair, and open." And Father Dan Danielson observed, "Given the times and given the bishop's background…he was much better than we had a right to expect and in some ways better than we deserved…In an age after the Second Vatican Council, an age where a lot of disruption has been possible, he stayed a positive middle course. That was no small accomplishment."

As Oakland's first bishop, Begin's openness, enthusiasm and personal warmth set the Diocese on the right course. The accomplishments and spirit of the Begin era would be embraced and built upon by his successor, native son, John S. Cummins.

Bishop Begin's funeral; Archbishop Joseph T. McGucken of San Francisco presides

ST. PETER MARTYR, PITTSBURG (1914)

St. Peter Martyr was established as a mission of the Dominican Fathers from Antioch in 1894. The second church was built in 1910 after the old wooden structure on Second Street burned following the 1906 earthquake. In 1914 it was raised to full parish status with Father Reginald Fei, OP, as the first pastor (1914-1920). The Dominican Fathers cared for the parish until 1966. In its early years, the parish was largely Italian, but in recent years it has become nearly 85% Latino along with Filipinos, Tongans, Italians and others. With a commitment to strong spirituality, education, evangelization and justice, the parish has developed extensive lay leadership with continuing education for its adults, youth and children. Its presence and active participation in the community contributes to the revitalization effort to the downtown area.

St. Lawrence O'Toole, Oakland, 1949 Confirmation with Bishop James O'Dowd in front of old church

The present pastor, Father Ricardo A. Chavez, is the first priestly vocation from this parish, ordained in 1963.

Mary Help of Christians was founded in 1915 as a Portuguese national parish. It is now a mission of St. Elizabeth and serves a predominantly Latino community.

ST. LAWRENCE O'TOOLE, OAKLAND (1916)

St. Lawrence is a vibrant parish situated in the foothills of Oakland. Founded as a mission of St. Jarlath in 1911, it was raised to parish status in 1916. For the first sixty years the parish consisted of Irish, Italian, Portuguese, and German American families. In recent decades the parish has enjoyed a great diversity, which includes many of the old families, as well as Latinos, Filipinos, African American, Asian, and multi-racial families. In 1949, the parish school was opened under the care of the Adrian Dominicans. It is currently run entirely by a lay staff, which continues the tradition of excellent education. Monsignors Leo J. Coughlin and Thaddeus Tillman served the parish for a combined total of 40 years. In 1957, a new church was built, which featured a gymnasium underneath. The gym has been the site of nonstop CYO action ever since.

Currently St. Lawrence is a loving, caring parish that features an active St. Vincent de Paul program, a beautiful choir, and a solid religious education program still directed by the Sisters of the Holy Family. In 2001, the St. Lawrence community welcomed the St. Cyril community to form St. Lawrence O'Toole-St. Cyril parish community.

MARY, HELP OF CHRISTIANS (1915)

ST. EDWARD, NEWARK (1920)

St. Edward's Parish in Newark became an established parish in 1920 with Father John Casey as the first pastor. At that time the parishioners were largely of Portuguese and Swiss descent, mostly engaged in dairy farming. In this 21st century, the parish numbers over 5,000 registered families consisting of Filipinos, Portuguese, Caucasian, Hispanics and Asians.

This bustling parish community puts great emphasis on the liturgy and its music ministry.

The Priests of the Society of the Precious Blood have administered St. Edward's since 1979.

Parade of parish organizations at picnic, 2000—Legion of Mary featured

ST. MARGARET MARY, OAKLAND (1922)

St. Margaret Mary, though small territorially, draws parishioners from a wide area. People come to the parish because of the beauty of the church and the dignity and solemnity of the liturgical celebrations. Mass is celebrated twice in English and twice in Latin on weekends. The 1962 Latin Mass is celebrated at 12:30, with the permission of the bishop. The Church's treasury of sacred music is a regular part of the worship.

St. Margaret Mary is a dedicated community with numerous educational and service programs. A major retrofitting of the church is nearing completion.

2001 RCIA class at Rite of Election

OUR LADY OF LOURDES, OAKLAND (1921)

On a sunny afternoon, March 27, 1772, Father Juan Crespi celebrated the first Mass in what is now Oakland. One hundred and forty-nine years later, on December 9, 1921, the parish of Our Lady of Lourdes was founded near that spot on the eastern shore of Lake Merritt. In 1924 the Sisters of the Holy Names established a school. It closed in 1989 due to insufficient enrollment. The parish, however, continues to be a vital presence in the lake area.

In order to stimulate lay involvement the parish liturgical committee went to work on re-configuring the worship space and parish plant. Today, "the parish is stronger and more devoted than ever". And it all began more than two centuries ago when Father Crespi first "held the host aloft and uttered the blessing".

Wedding in remodeled church

A Parish *Family Album*

ST. PATRICK, RODEO (1923)

Founded in 1923, the parish school was opened in 1956 under the Sisters of the Immaculate Heart of Mary. It is an ethnically mixed parish with a high percentage of Filipino parishioners.

QUEEN OF ALL SAINTS, CONCORD

Named after the original name of Concord, "Todos Santos," it was founded as a mission in 1876 and became a parish in 1923. In 1948, a school was established by the Sisters of St. Joseph of Carondelet. A new convent, rectory, and church were finished in the Marian year 1954, as "a gift of the people ...to our Lady."

First kindergarten class, 1955

ST. MARY MAGDALEN, BERKELEY (1923)

St. Mary Magdalen Parish was established in 1923 to serve the growing population of North Berkeley. Under the continuous guidance of the friars from the Western Dominican Province, and with dedicated lay Catholics, the parish remains a flourishing center of faith, worship and service for the residents of this interesting community. The Dominican Sisters of Mission San Jose established the School of the Madeleine in 1937, Kindergarten through eighth grade, which embodies the Dominican tradition of educational excellence. The renovated interior (1999) enhances the simple beauty of the California Mission-style church.

ST. THERESA, OAKLAND (1925)

St. Theresa's Parish was created in 1925, taking the eastern, uphill portions of Sacred Heart and St. Augustine parishes. It was one of the first parishes in the world to be named for the immensely popular new saint, St. Theresa of Lisieux, and for many years was known as the "Church of the Little Flower of Jesus". Milestones in parish history include the Oakland Firestorm of October 20, 1991, which destroyed the homes of 240 parish families, and the only visitation to the diocese of the relics of St. Theresa on their worldwide tour on January 19, 2000.

The parish has had only four pastors in its 76-year history. In 1958 St. Theresa School was opened, conducted by the Sisters of the Holy Names and remains a vital part of the parish.

St. Theresa Parish is known for its generosity to charitable causes such as St. Mary's Dining Room and Casa Vincentia. It also sponsors a Concern volunteer and a refuge in West Africa.

Close to 5,000 people from all over the Diocese came to welcome the visitation of the relics of St. Theresa on their worldwide tour. Pastor Monsignor Bernard Moran leads the veneration.

ST. PHILIP NERI, ALAMEDA (1925)

St. Philip Neri was established in 1925. The founding pastor was Father Maurice O'Keefe. Over the last seventy-six years, many wonderful transformations have taken place. Our school was established in 1959, conducted by the Sisters of Notre Dame de Namur. The school continues to provide our children with an atmosphere for spiritual growth, academic excellence, as well as physical and social development based on the teachings of Jesus Christ. The beautiful stained glass windows were installed to mark our 50th anniversary. They tell the story of the Creation of the world, the Passion, the Eucharist and Our Lord's Resurrection.

The parish is a tribute to the dedicated pastors, educators and parishioners of yesterday and today – who are responsible for building and shaping our Christian community.

ST. BARNABAS, ALAMEDA (1925)

St. Barnabas Parish has served the west end of Alameda for 77 years. From its beginning, the parish has incorporated people of many languages and backgrounds, drawing strength from their diverse heritages and bringing people together at the Lord's table. This parish's goals focus on family, life–long formation and stewardship. The Missionaries of the Precious Blood, to whom the parish has been entrusted since 1955, have shared their inclusive and generous spirituality with the parish community. We seek to incorporate the unique gifts of each member and empower all to share their gifts with the parish community and the community at large.

Easter vigil baptisms with Father Jeffrey Keyes, CPPS, at St. Barnabas, Alameda

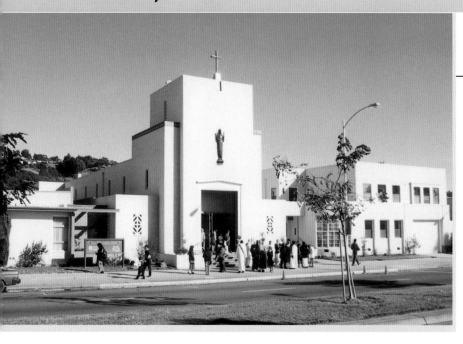

ST. JOHN THE BAPTIST, EL CERRITO (1925)

In 1925 St. John's was primarily Portuguese and Italian. In 2002 we celebrate a beautiful diverse community of 62 nationalities and cultures as the Body of Christ. Our hundreds of ministries have a strong emphasis on vibrant inclusive liturgies with a solid grounding in social justice, stewardship and care for the poor, e.g. Greater Richmond Interfaith Program, our Sister Parish in Haiti, a strong parochial school and youth ministry, etc.. St. John's in the 21st century is a church of many cultures and traditions, yet simultaneously one, as God is one—unity in diversity.

ST. JOHN THE BAPTIST, SAN LORENZO (1925)

St. John the Baptist Parish, currently a community of 2,100 families, was originally a mission of St. Leander Church in San Leandro and became a parish in 1925. Land was acquired and buildings erected to serve the growing parish. The parish plant consists of a church, rectory, school, playgrounds, community center and convent.

The parishioners of St. John's are the very essence of a true Christian community, full of care and concern for each other, not only in time of crises, but in everyday circumstances. They are a committed, faith-filled people who reach out to give and receive the love of fellow parishioners. This is evident in the ethnic diversity of the parish, and in an extensive lay ministry, which reflects the devotion of the parishioners.

ST. ANTHONY, OAKLEY (1925)

In 1906 land was donated to the Archdiocese of San Francisco to build a church in Oakley. The first Mass was offered in 1908 by the Dominican Fathers from Antioch, who took care of the faithful in this portion of Contra Costa County. There were many Portuguese immigrants from the Azores in this area. In 1925 the Parish of St. Anthony was established, administered by diocesan clergy. The founding pastor was Father Eugene Warren (1925-1930). A new church was built with parishioners volunteering their services. Other parish buildings were added. Bishop Hugh Donohoe, Auxiliary Bishop of San Francisco, dedicated the church on December 4, 1955.

The population in this part of Contra Costa County has exploded in the last few years, now numbering about 30,000 in Oakley and growing. The parish groups and services have tried to keep pace with this growth.

ST. CYRIL, OAKLAND (1926)

St. Andrew Kim Korean Pastoral Center - St. Cyril. Confirmation, May 19, 1991.

In a meeting called by Archbishop Edward J. Hanna in 1926, it was decided that there was a need in this area of East Oakland for a parish and school. The first church services and Masses were primarily for a European populace and were held in a donated theater, and later moved to a tent on the lot at 62nd Avenue. This was the first time since the 1906 earthquake that a tent was used for church services.

The first Mass in the new church was celebrated in October 1927, the same year the school opened its doors with a teaching faculty of Dominican Sisters. In 2001, the St. Andrew Kim Korean Pastoral Center assumed responsibility for the church.

CORPUS CHRISTI, PIEDMONT (1929):

Corpus Christi Parish was founded in 1929 to serve the affluent City of Piedmont. The first Mass was celebrated in a rented cottage. The permanent church was dedicated in 1936 and enlarged in 1962. The late Father Albano Oliveira (pastor, 1990-1998) began major renovation and retrofitting of the church and the construction of a community gathering space, the Gibson Center, which was completed in 1998. Corpus Christi School provides kindergarten through 8th grade education.

ST. BENEDICT, OAKLAND (1930)

St. Benedict Parish, nestled between the foothills and flatlands of East Oakland, has served an ethnically diverse community since its establishment in 1930. Presently with a majority African-American population, the leadership and liturgy reflects the spirituality of black culture and tradition of American Catholicism. Known for its hospitality, the parish has active civic, educational, ecumenical, and justice outreach to the wider community.

Rufus Fisher receives Pro Ecclesia et Pontifice Award, 2000; Odile Fisher, Father Jay Matthews, and Bishop Cummins take part in the ceremony

79

ST. JEROME, EL CERRITO (1941)

St. Jerome Parish on the Albany/Kensington border was established in 1941 to bridge the gap between St. Ambrose in Berkeley and St. John the Baptist in El Cerrito. Despite the rigors of the Second World War and the "wide open" nature of the suburban area, its founding pastor, Monsignor James Rohan, (1941-1973), succeeded in building a mission style church and, subsequently, a school (1955) and convent to care for the needs of an expanding populace. Nestled in the El Cerrito foothills, St. Jerome continues to provide a Catholic presence for Albany/Berkeley/Kensington residents.

Monsignor James Rohan with Sisters

ST. JOSEPH, PINOLE (1947)

Established as a mission in 1884, it did not become a parish until 1947. The school was founded in 1963 by the Sisters of St. Joseph, Third Order of St. Francis. It is an ethnically mixed parish with one of the largest Filipino communities in the diocese.

Montage with former pastor John J. Mallon featured

ST. MARY, WALNUT CREEK (1941)

St. Mary's Parish and the City of Walnut Creek have grown from a sleepy and small place to what is today a vibrant and bustling area. The little church had the distinction of having been a mission church of Sacred Heart, Oakland; St. Catherine of Siena, Martinez; and St. Isidore, Danville. Although Catholic presence in the area dates back to 1884, St. Mary's was not established as a parish until Father Louis Miller was named the first pastor in 1941. St. Mary's School (1960) and St. Mary's parish have always been a very important part of this busy, downtown parish.

SANTA MARIA, ORINDA (1947)

Marie Le Breton de LaVeaga was very concerned that there was no Catholic church in Orinda Park, the nearest one being Walnut Creek. With her own money she built a little chapel on her Estate. It came to be called Santa Maria, dedicated in 1896. The little wooden chapel continued to be used for many years. It accommodated 90 persons and a host of "termites, mice and the biggest spiders you ever saw". In later years, when larger facilities were needed for special occasions, the Orinda Country Club graciously permitted the use of their facilities.

A school was established in 1960, conducted by the Sisters of St. Joseph of Carondelet but closed in 1974. The school facilities were used for a time by St. Joseph School for the Deaf and Hard of Hearing.

The parish has embarked on a search for its history, to enhance its legacy in faith. The parishioners are being asked to contribute their "time, talent and treasure to continue to build upon that legacy".

Youth Confirmation Retreat 2000

OUR LADY OF GRACE, CASTRO VALLEY (1947)

By 1947. the chicken ranches and orchards of Castro Valley had been supplemented by suburban development that required the establishment of the first parish in that growing community. In 1948 the church was constructed followed by other parochial buildings. Our Lady of Grace School was established in 1955, conducted by the Carmelite Sisters of Christian Charity. Diocesan priests staffed the parish until 1980 when the Augustinians arrived to take over the parish and under their direction the school and parish have continued to flourish. This is a very busy parish with many and varied ministries to serve a community of older parishioners and new incoming young families.

IMMACULATE HEART OF MARY, BRENTWOOD (1949)

Immaculate Heart of Mary Parish was established in 1949. In September of the same year, the charming white stucco church was dedicated. Several parishioners donated items such as the carved wooden altar, bell, and golden tabernacle. The parishioners were very generous with their time and talents as well.

The current make-up of the parish is about 50 % English-speaking, 45% Spanish-speaking. Recently retired pastor Father John Garcia, (1984-2002), worked on the Spanish Mission Band.

A Parish
Family Album

OUR LADY OF THE ROSARY, UNION CITY (1951)

Before 1907, the Catholics of the area of what is now Union City, attended Mass in Niles (Fremont). In 1907 Mass was celebrated in a hall owned by Albert Silva at 10th and I St. That building was destroyed by fire. A Mission Church was built on 13th and H Streets in 1907. It was also destroyed by fire in 1952, so Mass was celebrated in the new Parish Hall which had been dedicated 10 days earlier. It was not until 1951 that Our Lady of the Rosary became a parish. The present church was dedicated on March 12, 1960. The bell tower was added in 1964. St. Anne in the Alvarado District was a mission of Our Lady of the Rosary until 1973. The Parish school was added.

The Franciscan Fathers administered the parish from 1961 to 1971 when diocesan priests were once again assigned to the parish. Our Lady of the Rosary has a large Spanish-speaking population.

ASSUMPTION, SAN LEANDRO (1951)

The gifts of the Holy Spirit abound when you simply say Yes and the people of the Parish of the Assumption have consistently said Yes! As a result, the gifts have been abundant. As we the parish celebrated its past 50 years, we look forward to the future in which the parish community, our church and each of us must continue to say Yes! We must be confident that the gifts of Christ's love and the Holy Spirit will guide, inspire and touch us.

The parish was established in 1951 in response to the influx of many new families following World War II and now serves about 1,200 families.

Rosary makers at Assumption, San Leandro

CHRIST THE KING, PLEASANT HILL (1951)

Father Brian Joyce with "original" parishioners, 2001. These parishioners were present at the parish's founding in 1951.

We Remember .. We Celebrate .. We Believe ... is the motto of this parish. With the cooperation of energetic parishioners, a quality that continues to describe the people of Christ the King Parish, within two months after its founding, the first parish Mass was celebrated on Easter Sunday in a chapel complete with a striped tent! A school and other parish buildings were added.

The third pastor (1962-1988), the much loved Monsignor James Wade, fashioned and guided the parish for twenty-six years with his faith, strength and gentle humor. Father Brian Joyce, the present pastor, writes: "Our parish journey includes prayer and counseling, moments of joy and moments of grief. Together we have sought to come together to praise our God, share our faith and care for those in need. The journey goes on and we do not forget; We remember, We celebrate, We Believe".

ST. CLEMENT, HAYWARD (1951)

The parish was erected in 1951. In 1959 a school was added with Sisters of St. Joseph of Wichita. The Holy Cross Fathers administered the parish from 1980 until 2001. Mass is celebrated in Spanish each weekend.

ST. PERPETUA, LAFAYETTE (1952)

Nestled in the beautiful hillsides of Lafayette, where it was established in 1952, St. Perpetua Parish is a hidden treasure. It is not easy to find our campus of church, school and offices – located as we are in the midst of a quiet neighborhood off the beaten path. Once you find us, however, and experience the charm of the Lamorinda area, you discover a welcoming, enthusiastic and caring community. We are rebuilding ourselves at the end of our half-century mark and at the beginning of a new millennium. As our Mission Statement proclaims: "Our communion with Jesus and with the Church binds us together through times of transition and growth." Today is a time for both!

ST. JOACHIM, HAYWARD (1951)

The parish was established in 1951. Benedictine Sisters of Mt. Angel taught at the school, opened in 1958. The parish has a very large Latino population and other ethnic communities as well.

THE ERA OF JOHN CUMMINS

More importantly, his appointment suggested that the Diocese of Oakland would stay on the progressive trajectory established by Bishop Begin. In addition, Cummins was an immensely likable figure, who, like his predecessor, had a warm smile and approachable style. *The Voice* provided an apt description of Cummins as a "friendly, open, humorous, intellectual and priestly man." Over the course of the next twenty-five years, the bishop would become deeply loved for demonstrating these virtues in his episcopal office.

John Stephen Cummins was born on March 3, 1928 at Providence Hospital in Oakland. He grew up in Berkeley, attending St. Augustine's Elementary School. At the age of 13, he entered the minor seminary at St. Joseph's College in Mountain View to study for the priesthood for the Archdiocese of San Francisco. He completed his studies at St. Patrick's Seminary in Menlo Park, and was ordained to the priesthood January 24, 1953 at St. Mary's Cathedral by Bishop Hugh A. Donohoe. He first served as associate pastor of Mission Dolores, while also

Oakland was delighted to learn that Bishop Begin's successor was to be one of its own, Bishop John S. Cummins, who was appointed May 3, 1977, shortly after Begin's death.

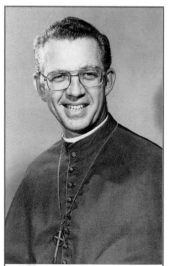

Bishop John S. Cummins

serving as campus minister for San Francisco State College. In 1957 he became an instructor at Bishop O'Dowd High School in Oakland, serving as Dean of Boys as well.

In 1962, when the Diocese of Oakland was established, Cummins was named the diocese's first Chancellor, a position he held until 1971. In February 1971, he became the Executive Director of the newly created California Catholic Conference of Bishops in Sacramento. Three years later he was appointed auxiliary bishop of Sacramento and was ordained at the Memorial Auditorium in Sacramento on May 16, 1974 by Bishop Alden Bell of Sacramento with Bishops Hugh Donohoe and Floyd Begin assisting. Following Bishop Begin's death, Cummins was appointed the second bishop of Oakland.

His installation took place on June 30, 1977 at the Oakland Civic Auditorium Arena, and was a gala event. Apostolic Delegate Jean Jadot presided. Wiley Manuel, the first African American California Supreme Court Justice and a parishioner at St. Paschal's, read the first reading. The many

St. Joseph the Worker in Berkeley, provided "sanctuary" for refugees who lacked proper documentation. Protests against US policies in Central America continued through the 1980s.

Congresses on Peace and Justice

By 1982, thirty percent of the parishes in the diocese had social concerns committees. In 1985, an "ad hoc" committee of laity and religious gathered the committees together in what became an annual congress on peace and justice.

In 1989, the diocese established a Social Action Resource Center through Diocesan Catholic Charities. Bishop Cummins emphasis was once again on education; action was left to the local level.

The Oakland Community Organization(OCO)

One of the major practical developments in the struggle for social justice at the local level in Oakland was the creation of the Oakland Community Organization. Though not directly a program of the diocese, the local church was instrumental in its creation and success. In 1972, Father Oliver Lynch of St. Elizabeth's parish in Oakland invited Jesuit Fathers John Baumann and Jerry Helfrich, trained in the Saul Alinsky school of community organizing, to come to Oakland to begin some grass roots organizing. On November 17, 1972, the two priests opened the Oakland Training Institute (OTI) in East Oakland. Within two years of its establishment, the OTI had helped establish seven community organizations. In the early years, the OTI concentrated on neighborhood organizing, and focused on neighborhood issues. The first issues were relatively simple and intensely local. One participant recalls that the first issue addressed in her neighborhood was the problem of stray dogs.

The OTI program required the organizers to go from door to door to meet and talk to the people of the area. The organizers then hosted a neighborhood meeting, where common concerns could be discussed, an issue identified, and specific actions planned.

Part of the genius of the OTI method was the development of local leaders. One St. Elizabeth's parishioner, Fran Matarrese, came to chair the East Oakland Housing Committee, which addressed the problem of affordable housing in the Fruitvale area, and pushed to have vacant buildings rehabilitated.

St. Elizabeth's, which was the host parish of the OTI, often provided its facilities for meetings with city officials. In 1976, five Oakland neighborhood groups conducted public hearings at St. Elizabeth's on recreation, housing, employment, crime, and neighborhood development.

Oakland Community Organization Convention

89

The hearings were an important step on the way to the creation of OCO.

In 1977, an umbrella group called the All Oakland Organization was developed to help organize all the local neighborhood groups. On May 14, 1977 a community convention was held at Merritt College, and was attended by neighborhood clubs, area organizations, merchant groups, and the OTI. The All Oakland Organization, which came to be called the Oakland Community Organization, was to provide "a forum on city-wide problems." The smaller groups would maintain their identity, while participating in the larger OCO to combat larger problems.

In 1985, the OCO experimented with a new approach and began organizing through parishes and congregations rather than through neighborhoods. The parish base enabled the groups to move beyond the neighborhood, while still incorporating neighborhood concerns; the parish organization also provided a more stable base. Many parishes, particularly in the Flatlands, actively participated.

The key to OCO success has been its ability to empower people to take control of their own neighborhoods, and to enable them to influence city policy.

CONSULTATION AND PARTICIPATION: THE OAKLAND STYLE

During Bishop Cummins' tenure, Oakland became known for its participatory and consultative style. The impetus for this did not begin with Cummins but was found in the Second Vatican Council. The Council called for broader consultation at the diocesan level, and stressed a new watchword—"shared responsibility;" it called for the creation of diocesan Senates to give "effective assistance to the bishop in the governance of his diocese."

Priests Senate, 1970-71

The first Priests' Senate for the Diocese of Oakland was formed in October 1966, with Father Augustine J. Quinan elected its first president. Over the next three decades, the senate underwent a series of metamorphoses, until the current Presbyteral Council was put in place in the mid 1990s.

Whatever form the Priests Senate took, it was the primary advisory body to the bishop, and was instrumental in constructing diocesan policy. The Senate has initiated such important diocesan projects as the study of women in ministry and the creation of the Diocesan Pastoral Council to name just two.

Parish Councils

Shared responsibility also applied to the parish level. Pastors were encouraged, and later mandated, to establish parish councils to assist them in the governance of the parish. St. Leonard's in Fremont under pastor Martin Walsh established the first parish council in the diocese in 1965. As one parish representative observed, "There are not too many priests who have the courage to actually involve laymen... and women... to tell them how to run the parish."

By 1968, twenty-five parishes had councils, but the notion of laymen telling "them how to run the parish" caused many pastors to hesitate. Even Bishop Begin began to doubt the wisdom of councils even though he had mandated them. According to Margaret Mealey, Begin stopped the development of the councils because several "weren't working within the institution," but instead were working to "sidestep the bishop or pastor."

First Diocesan Pastoral Council

One of the most active and effective parish councils was operating out of St. Elizabeth's parish, though the council may have seemed too radical for some pastors. As the parish bulletin put it, "A parish council is the extension of the democratic process to the parish." The success of St. Elizabeth's Parish Council encouraged council members to share the fruit of their experience with other parishes. On May 12, 1973 the Council initiated, organized and directed a diocesan-wide parish council convention held at St. Elizabeth's. The organizers promised "a free flow of ideas." Under the acronym SURE--Support, Unity, Recognition, and Education--various issues were discussed that directly affected parish life. Each parish was invited to send two representatives; about 145 people from 33 parishes attended. Two problems recurred: recalcitrant pastors and a lack of initiative. The following year, under the direction of Cliff Pletschet, a second convention was held with the theme, "The People Are the Church." The free flow of ideas was too much for Bishop Begin who wrote the convention's organizers telling them to take the money in their treasury and "give yourselves a going away party because you are going away." Thus, the great parish convention experiment came to an end. The Diocese of Oakland was not ready for too much democracy.

[By 2000, nearly every parish had initiated a parish council, with the formation of councils given a real boost by the efforts of Chuck Siebenand, Director of Pastoral Planning].

Diocesan Pastoral Council

By 1981, things had changed. The Priests Senate, at the prodding of Father Brian Joyce, began discussing the possibility of developing a diocesan pastoral council to serve as a consultative body to the bishop, to provide a different perspective from that of the Priests Senate. Broader consultation was sought. In 1983, the Senate affirmed the creation of a pastoral council that was to be elected at an historic diocesan convention. In early 1984, an Office of the Diocesan Pastoral Council was established under the direction of Mark Fischer with Sister Marcia Frideger, working as a consultant. A major convention was planned in November to establish direction, goals, and priorities for the diocese.

On the weekend of November 2-4, 1984, after almost three years of discussion, more than 350 delegates from 87 parishes met at Holy Names College for the historic first Diocesan Pastoral Convention. Chairing the convention was Chancellor Father George Crespin. The convention crackled with excitement, and according to *Voice* editor Dan Morris, "an almost festive spirit" prevailed. Delegates knew they were about something important. The convention opened with an address by Bishop Cummins, who told the gathered delegates the convention was an opportunity for "consultation," "subsidiarity" and "discernment." After three days of heady exchange, the convention approved a tentative Mission Statement: "United by one Lord, one faith, one Baptism, we, the Catholic people of the Diocese of Oakland, affirm the Church's universal mission as it has been announced in every time and place. Our mission is that of Jesus… to proclaim the good news of salvation in word and deed, to worship the Father and celebrate his saving action in the sacraments…"

The convention reconvened on the weekend of January 11-13, 1985 to finish its work. Again a spirit of excitement and openness prevailed. The convention elected the first Diocesan Pastoral Council—14 members where elected while the Chancellor, Vicar General and President of the Priests' Senate were members *ex officio*. The convention also voted for the top five diocesan priorities which they listed as 1) formation of lay leadership; 2) youth/young adult ministry; 3) social justice; 4) education, and 5) evangelization. Other concerns included outreach to the poor and disadvantaged, parish councils, vocations, spiritual renewal, and family life. In every category, the ethnic and cultural diversity of the diocese was to be emphasized.

On March 2, 1985 the Diocesan Pastoral Council met for the first time. Their mandate was to study the five goals defined by the convention, and to suggest ways to achieve those goals. Five committees were established, one for each goal. An Executive Committee consisting of Gesine Laufenberg, Priscilla Scotlan, and Father Dan Danielson was also formed. In early 1987, the Council presented its report for implementation, "To Undertake Our Mission." With the work of the first Council completed, a second convention began to be planned.

On the weekend of January 29-30, 1988, the second Diocesan Pastoral Convention was held at Holy Names College with Father George Crespin once again presiding. The follow-up weekend was held on February 26-28. The second convention elected a new Diocesan Pastoral Council with Zelda Humphrey elected as chair. Its most important work came in defining what it called "The Ten Essentials of Parish Life." The Ten Essentials included quality liturgy, good leadership, outreach to the poor, evangelization, spirituality, small communities, diversity of cultures, sense of belonging, involvement-participation-inclusion, and formation.

The work of the second Diocesan Pastoral Council was concluded in 1990. It was hoped that the implementation of the Ten Essentials would revitalize parish life.

First Diocesan Pastoral Convention voting

HISTORIC EVENTS

RCIA: Rite of Election, 1981

Under Bishop Cummins direction, the diocese has been at the forefront of the new Rite of Christian Initiation for Adults (RCIA). In Lent, 1981, a diocesan-wide Rite of Election was held at St. Francis de Sales with Bishop Cummins presiding. All who were in preparation for Baptism, or reception into the Catholic Church through parish RCIA programs, were welcomed by Bishop Cummins. Since then, the Rite of Election has been held annually, and has become one of the most popular events in the Diocese.

*Pope John
Paul II at
Candlestick
Park,
San
Francisco*

Jubilee 1987

On June 27, more than 5,000 people gathered at Laney College and the Kaiser Convention Center in Oakland for a day-long celebration of the 25th anniversary of the Diocese and the 10th anniversary of Bishop Cummins as bishop. The celebration featured a wide variety of entertainments including ethnic dancers, choirs, foods, a "Divine Comedy Revue," a parade of parishes, and a major concert. The day ended with a candlelight procession from the Convention Center to Channel Park, concluding with a fireworks display. As was becoming increasingly customary at diocesan events, the cultural diversity of the diocese was fully displayed and celebrated.

Papal Visit 1987

In September 1987, the Bay Area was treated to the dynamic presence and holiness of Pope John Paul II. Though the pope did not come to Oakland, thousands from the diocese journeyed to either Monterey or San Francisco to greet the pontiff. On September 18, thousands of Oaklanders joined more than 60,000 people at Candlestick Park in San Francisco for Mass with Pope John Paul. Joining the cry, "John Paul Two, We Love You," the day was most memorable for all who attended.

Cathedral tower after the 1989 earthquake

The Earthquake of 1989

Not all the events of the late 1980s were so positive. On October 17, 1989 as the Bay Area prepared for the third game of baseball's World Series featuring the Oakland Athletics and the San Francisco Giants, the Bay Area was rocked by the Loma Prieta Earthquake that registered 7.1 on the Richter scale. The most significant damage in Oakland was the collapse of the Cypress structure in West Oakland, a portion of the 880 freeway. Father Tony Dummer, OMI, of St. Mary-Immaculate Conception rushed to the scene and anointed two of the victims. Parishioners from St. Patrick's and St. Columba's joined the rescue efforts, as did many others. Catholic Charities and the local Catholic food kitchens did their part to provide relief. The old Mercy Manor, a vacant convalescent home was reopened as a "temporary residence for the elderly and disabled." Bishop Cummins was in San Diego for a meeting of the California Catholic Bishops at the time of the quake. He rushed home to be with the people of Oakland. He noted, "The human tragedy is our prime concern."

Cathedral is knocked down

While Oakland mourned the victims of the quake, Bishop Cummins learned that two of the diocese's most venerable churches had been severely damaged: Sacred Heart Church in Oakland, and the Cathedral, St. Francis de Sales. Cummins went to Sacred Heart and assured the people, "You will continue to exist. We will rebuild." Initial damage reports indicated that rebuilding would be expensive—estimates for repair ran at over $4 million for Sacred Heart and over $6 million for the Cathedral. After extensive

Lifting the top off Sacred Heart

consultation, the diocese decided not to rebuild either church. Besides the expense, it was determined that even if the structures were rebuilt they would not necessarily be safe during the next earthquake. Some protested the decision, and preservationists mobilized to preserve the historic structures. After a protracted legal battle, both structures were ultimately torn down. Since then, Sacred Heart has built a new church, dedicated in 1998, and the Cathedral parish has merged with St. Mary's Immaculate Conception in 1993. In 2000, planning for a new Cathedral began.

The Firestorm of 1991

Almost exactly two years later, Oakland was devastated by another catastrophe. On Sunday, October 20, 1991 a fire in the Oakland hills burned out of control, turning into a firestorm that left more than 25 dead, 150 injured, more than 3,000 homes destroyed and 1,600 acres burned. St. Theresa's parish was hardest hit with close to 50 percent of its parishioners losing their homes. Miraculously, all the parish buildings survived. Monsignor Bernard Moran performed heroically, watering the buildings throughout the day, until finally being evacuated by the police and fire departments at 9:30 in the evening.

As the fire was starting to spread, Bishop Cummins was on his way to install Father William

The firestorm takes off, 1991
(Photo courtesy of Oakland Public History Room)

Survivors embrace in wake of firestorm (Chris Duffey photo)

Aftermath of the firestorm (Chris Duffey photo)

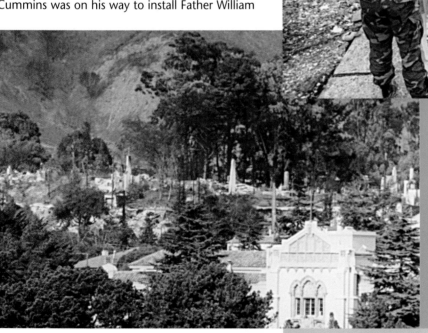

Macchi as pastor at St. Francis of Assisi in Concord. He was one of the last cars through the Caldecott Tunnel and he witnessed the fire on the crest of the hill. The next day Bishop Cummins visited the relief shelters, meeting many parishioners and providing solace. On October 24, "an emotion filled Mass" was offered for the victims and their families at St. Leo's Church. The following Sunday, October 27, Bishop Cummins celebrated an equally emotional healing Mass at St. Theresa's Church. The Bishop reflected, "It is a healing, not just of the evil, but also the hurt, the puzzlement, the anger and resentment of suffering that comes to innocent people. Part of the healing is the insight of faith; somehow, there is a redemptive element in suffering." The Bishop was deeply moved by one survivor who told him simply, "One has to detach oneself from material possessions… The family is safe."

As had been the case in the earthquake, Catholic Charities and local parishes responded generously during the crisis.

STRATEGIC PLANNING PROCESS

Like many other major initiatives in the history of the diocese, the move toward a strategic plan originated in the Priests Senate. The Senate realized, however, that strategic planning could not be limited to the Senate—the entire diocese had to become involved. With that in mind, Bishop Cummins, with the support of his Chancellor, Father Raymond Breton, initiated a strategic planning process for the diocese, which he placed under the direction of Father Richard Mangini. According to Mangini, the process was to prepare the Church in Oakland for the third millennium; "to determine what kind of Church we want to be in 2000." Of particular concern was the rapid population growth in the diocese, particularly in northern and eastern Contra Costa County and southern and southeastern Alameda County, as farmland was converted into housing. Equally pressing was the increasing flow of immigrants to the diocese. The growth continued at a time when the diocese was increasingly hard pressed for funds. Thus, one mandate of the Process was to ask, "how to use all our resources well and effectively."

The diocese adopted as a model the process and structures suggested by the Chicago-based Center for Parish Development, with the Center's Paul Dietterich hired as a consultant. The first step was to create an objective profile of the diocese, review the diocese's goals, ministries, and finances, and then strategize as how to improve and develop the diocese. Mangini acknowledged that the difficulty was to "envision the future," while "concretizing the present." A Strategic Planning Council (SPC) was appointed, and the process begun. Focus groups were formed within each parish in the hopes of getting a clear picture of the diocese.

By 1991, certain problems were becoming clear. The initial study indicated that the diocese was increasingly split into two dioceses—one in the inner cities and one in the suburbs. At the same time the Council suggested the diocese had failed to adequately engage the non-Anglo population. Though the diocese was committed to developing into a truly multicultural church, Diocesan Pastoral Council member Catalina Esquivel observed, "The change to a real multicultural church will not be easy; its implications for the future have got to be worked out."

By 1992, the SPC presented the bishop with fifteen "challenges" that faced the diocese. On May 4, 1992 Bishop Cummins issued an important wide-ranging pastoral letter entitled "Signposts Pointing to the Future." Cummins used the occasion of the diocese's thirtieth anniversary to review its past and set forth the challenges that confronted the diocese in the future. The challenges were presented under four general areas: **A. The Church as the People of God:** 1. Discovering our role as stewards; 2. Diversity, discrimination, sexism and racism in the Church; 3. The Family and the Changing nature of society; 4. Youth. **B. The Church as Communion in the Spirit:** 5. Lifelong spiritual formation; 6. Liturgical formation; 7. Role and future of Catholic schools. **C. The Church as Those Who Reach Out to Others:** 8. Ecumenism and cooperation with other religions; 9. Evangelization; 10. Policy and commitment of the diocese to the inner city and areas of economic decline. 11. Service and advocacy for social justice and human rights. **D. The Church as the Community That is Organized and Visible:** 12. Accountability: managing and developing resources; 13. Lay leadership recognition and development within the church; 14. New structures and models for parish life; 15. Pastoral leadership.

To confront the challenges Action Planning Groups were established to "open up" each challenge and present recommendations.

Bishop Cummins then proceeded to paint his own vision of the future Church in Oakland in which he reaffirmed the diocese's traditional participatory style. Highlighting responsibility, freedom, participation and initiative, he stressed dialogue. "A necessary accompaniment of both responsibility and initiative is the role of dialogue. Those affected by a decision must be allowed a say in the forming of that decision. Consultation out of respect for the presence of the Spirit and the gifts of the people becomes a requirement." Bishop then stressed the three essentials necessary in confronting the future—Prayer, Community and Service. In typical Cummins' fashion, the letter ended on a positive upbeat note, indicating that though there were many challenges ahead, he concluded "… from the strength that comes from the central truths of our historical tradition… we can look to the future with hope."

By October 1993, the committees made their final recommendations to the bishop. Included were several specific recommendations: promote "small participatory communities in all parishes," promote the spirituality of stewardship, develop a school for training lay leaders, create a task force to strengthen Catholic schools, and redefine the role of the local deaneries. The final report was issued in March 1994 as "Faith in Service to the World," and was accepted by Bishop Cummins in April. Seven task forces were created: Deanery, Personnel Placement, Communications, Consultative Bodies, Reconstructing Parish Life, Authority of School Superintendent, Faith and Formation Ministry. Fathers Richard Mangini, Paul Vassar, and George Crespin, with Sister Barbara Thiella, were appointed to implement the plan.

Implementing the Pastoral Plan

The implementation has met with some early successes. First, the Bishop's Administrative Council (BAC) was restructured to make it more efficient and more responsive to parishes. Second, the size of the deaneries was decreased, and the deaneries reorganized to make them more effective.

School of Pastoral Ministry

One of the recommendations called for a school for training lay ministers. Several previous attempts had been made to provide for adult education. In 1967, Father Brian Joyce had been appointed the diocese's first director of adult education. The response to his early efforts was tremendous as crowds in excess of 600 people attended lectures. Later in 1986, the diocese sponsored the Jordan Institute, a two-year program for parish ministers. In 1995, under the direction of Monsignor Ted Kraus, the diocese began an Institute for Ministerial Training that came to be known as the School of Pastoral Ministry, a three-year program designed to provide training for lay leaders. The first class assembled had more than 100 students. At the same time, a program was developed for Spanish-speaking ministers under the direction of Carlos Rivas—La Escuela de Ministerios Pastorales. An earlier program, the Instituto Tepeyac had been formed in 1991.

RENEW

One of the recommendations of the SPP had been the creation of small participatory communities within parishes. To achieve this goal, the diocese sponsored RENEW. RENEW was a program for spiritual renewal that was based on the development of small, faith sharing communities. The program had originated in the Archdiocese of Newark, and had spread across the country. Father Dan Danielson of St. Augustine's in Pleasanton brought the idea to the diocese in 1983, but, at that time, Bishop Cummins felt the diocese was not ready for it, as the diocese already had too many other programs operating. Undeterred, Danielson began the program in his own community in conjunction with two neighboring parishes, St. Charles and St. Michael of Livermore. The response in the three parishes was overwhelming with more than 1200 people participating. The program ran from 1986 to 1988. When it was over, St. Augustine built on the small communities that had been formed and created a new concept of parish organization— neighborhood Christian communities.

With the success at St. Augustine's and the recommendation of the SPP, the diocese undertook RENEW in 1995. Nora Petersen, who had run St. Augustine's program, was hired to direct the program. It was enormously successful. Over the course of three years, more than 85 percent of the parishes in the diocese participated; more than 17,000 people joined over 2,000 small groups. Many long-lasting faith communities were developed. Three years after the conclusion of the program, more than 1,000 small faith communities still meet regularly. Many

believe small Christian communities are the future of the Church.

Consultative Bodies

The consultative style so encouraged by the diocese and endorsed by the SPP, was further developed in the late 1990s. The Priests Senate, now called the Presbyteral Council, continued to play a major role in the direction of the diocese. In 1998, a new Diocesan Pastoral Council was formed to serve as the "main planning group" of the diocese, and to specifically address "pastoral needs." In 2000, a Deacons' Council was formed to insure the input of the growing permanent diaconate community. But the most significant development was the creation of the Lay Ecclesial Ministers Council, established in 1999.

One of the key features of the post Vatican II Church was the explosion of lay ministries and lay ministers, with many lay ministers working full or part time for parishes or the diocese. In 1980, the US Bishops in a document entitled "Called and Gifted," used the term "lay ecclesial minister" for the first time to designate this new minister. As the number of lay ministers in the diocese grew, a number of lay ecclesial ministers gathered together in the Fall of 1996 for mutual support, but also to address such common concerns as wages, working conditions, and professional development. An ad hoc working group was formed to study the issues at greater depth with Kelly O'Lague Dulka, the Director of Religious Education at Our Lady of Grace in Castro Valley, and Steve Mullin, pastoral associate at St. Joseph's in Alameda, providing leadership. At the prodding of Ken Reggio of the Bishop's Administrative Council, the working group was encouraged to develop a proposal to create a consultative body of lay ecclesial ministers to be given official status. Thus in April 1999, Bishop Cummins appointed the first Lay Ecclesial Ministers Council as an official advisory body, the first of its kind anywhere in the United States.

Beyond that the Council provides "a forum for the ongoing support and formation of lay ministers." The National Association of Lay Ministry acknowledged the special contribution of Oakland by giving the Council a special award in 2001. It claimed, "It is the first of its kind in the country where lay ecclesial ministers have been placed in an official consultative capacity to their bishop within the structure of the diocese."

Decline in Clergy

While lay ministry was increasing, the number of ordained clergy continued to dwindle. In addition, the population of Alameda and Contra Costa Counties had nearly doubled between 1964 and 1999 from 1.2 million to 2.3 million. On November 21, 1999 Bishop Cummins issued a letter to be read at all parishes throughout the diocese, in which he alerted the faithful to the growing crisis—parishes might have to be merged, and every parish might not be able to have a resident priest. Over the course of the previous fifteen years, the diocese had experimented with new forms of parish leadership. In 1984, Sister Marie Wiedner was made administrator of St. Charles in Livermore, the first non-ordained person to head a parish, but only for a three month period as the pastor was on sabbatical. In 1986, Penny Pendola and Father Leo Edgerly, Jr, were appointed co-administrators of St. Paschal's in Oakland. In 1989, she became sole administrator as well as serving as school principal. In 1996, Catherine McGhee was appointed administrator, (now dubbed "Parish Life Director") of St. Monica's in Moraga after serving as pastoral associate for ten years. Deacon George Peters was named administrator of St. Alphonsus Ligouri in San Leandro in 1998. In addition, Sister Marian Wright, SNJM was appointed Parish Life Director at St. Andrew-St. Joseph in 2000, and layman Stephen Mullin was appointed the same for All Saints in Hayward in 2001.

Permanent Diaconate

The ancient office of deacon was re-established by the Second Vatican Council, and the US Bishops approved the ordination of married deacons by the early 1970s. The move to establish the permanent diaconate in Oakland originated with the Priests Senate in 1973, though the idea was promoted by the Black Catholic Caucus. It was hoped that the diaconate would provide a means of creating greater minority representation in leadership positions in the diocese. A study committee was formed and the program was approved in June 1974 by the Senate and Bishop Begin. On October 4, 1975 the first deacon class was accepted for candidacy at St. Francis de Sales Cathedral. Formation was completed under the direction of Fathers James Schexnayder and Dan Danielson. On February 17, 1978 the first deacon class of twenty-seven men was ordained. Since then four additional classes have been ordained, and more than 100 deacons have provided distinguished service to the diocese. Though the deacon is most recognized for his service in the ministry of the altar, his essential task is service to the poor and needy, to be a "voice for the voiceless," in the diocese. Deacons have contributed outstanding service in prison ministry, hospital ministry, ethnic ministry, soup kitchens, social justice and a variety of other arenas.

Episcopal Converts

The diocese has also benefited from the conversion of several Episcopal priests. The first was Ron Atwood, ordained in 1984. In 1990, David Staal, another convert, was ordained at St. Augustine's in Pleasanton, making him "the first married Catholic priest to serve in Northern California."

Conclusion

As the diocese enters the third millennium it confronts many challenges. Most pressing, however, is a challenge it has long confronted—the challenge of creating a multicultural Church.

CHAPTER

8

ONE FAITH, MANY CULTURES

In 1965, the United States government passed an immigrant reform act that set off a new wave of immigration. The immigrants that have arrived since 1965 have come from far different points of origin than the earlier immigrants. Prior to 1965, more than 60% of all immigrants to the United States came from Europe. After 1965, more than 80% of all immigrants came from Asia, Mexico, Central and South America. This was especially true in the Diocese of Oakland. By the late 1980s, a majority of immigrants to the diocese were coming from Asia, with the Philippine immigrants the most numerous. Substantial numbers continued to come from Mexico as well. The large influx of immigrants dramatically changed the make-up of the diocese. By 2000, ethnic minorities were now the majority, with Latinos representing the largest group. In Catholic schools, ethnic minorities were also the majority, with well over 50% of Catholic school students belonging to ethnic minorities.

The transition to a multi-ethnic, multicultural Church has not been without its problems, but the diocese has determined to treat the new groups as "gifts, not as problems." In January 1994 the diocese celebrated "Immigrant Celebration Sunday" in which Bishop Cummins reminded the people of their immigrant roots,

The Diocese of Oakland has always been an immigrant church, in which many cultures have come together to form the People of God.

"We, as a Catholic people particularly, should be characterized as welcoming. We are aware that like so many who came to America, we were treated at least with ambivalence. Many of our parents and grandparents can remember unacceptance." It was not to be that way in Oakland.

Cummins' predecessor, Bishop Begin, had set the tone by establishing vicariates for the various cultural groups. In 1984, the Office of Ethnic Ministries was established with a new approach: vicariates were replaced by ethnic pastoral centers, which were established for each group to assist them in celebrating and maintaining their faith. Since 1984, the Office of Ethnic Ministries has benefited from the astute guidance and leadership of Sister Felicia Sarati, CSJ. Sister's vision has been one of deep respect for the different cultures, but it also includes a desire to inspire in each group an appreciation of their place within the larger Church.

In the 1980s, in order to gather the different cultures together, several multicultural Marian days were celebrated, the first at St. Joseph's in Alameda in 1986. Prayers were offered in Spanish, Portuguese, Chinese, Tagalog, Korean, Vietnamese, and English. On August 14, 1988, a

Most significant, however, were the efforts of Father Clarence Howard, SVD, named pastor of St. Patrick's in West Oakland in 1964. Before being assigned to Oakland, Father Howard, a native of North Carolina, served in Mississippi and Louisiana. Coming from the overt racism of the South, Father Howard was disappointed in what he found in Oakland, "Though I expected to find a healthy racial climate here, those expectations did not long survive in West Oakland." With others he joined the struggle in reversing centuries old attitudes.

In the early 1970s, greater emphasis was placed on African American self-determination in society and in the church. In 1971, Morris Soublet, Sr., of St. Andrew-St. Joseph, and George Scotlan of Sacred Heart attended a national conference of Black Catholics in the East. When they returned, with the strong support of Rose Casanave and Isabelle Boutte Kellum, plans were initiated to establish a Bay Area Black Catholic Caucus. On February 5-6, 1972 the Knights and Ladies of St. Peter Claver sponsored the first pastoral conference on Black Catholicism in the diocese entitled "Liberation and Love" and held at Merritt College—more than 150 attended. In conjunction with the conference, a "Mass for Black Unity" was celebrated at St. Columba's, with Congressman Ronald Dellums in attendance (Dellums had received his grade school education at St. Patrick's). The conference explored such crucial issues as racism within the church, the need for more African American clergy and leaders, and the development of an authentic "black liturgy."

1972 ended with an historic Black Catholic Eucharistic celebration at the Cathedral in Oakland on Christmas Eve. Behind the altar a twenty-foot tapestry of a Black Madonna was unfurled.

Mass for Black Unity at St. Columba, 1972

Father James Goode, OFM, at Black Catholic Revival, 1981

Morris Soublet and George Scotlan prepare for Black Catholic Lay Caucus

The same year, the Bay Area Black Catholic Caucus was formed, and realtor John Guillory of St. Benedict's parish was elected its first president. A Stanford graduate, Guillory briefly played pro football. He noted, "The need here is to develop ideologies which reflect both American and Black hopes and experiences." In a similar vein, Father Jay Matthews, who in 1974 became the first African American priest to be ordained in northern California, asserted the Caucus was "to strengthen the identity of Black Catholics in the Church," and to "move from the fringe of the Church to its mainstream." Again and again, the Caucus stressed the need for African Americans to be involved in diocesan decision making, and the need for African American priests and pastoral ministers. The Caucus played an important role in encouraging the diocese to develop the permanent diaconate in the hope that African American deacons would provide new models of pastoral leadership in the diocese. In 1978, Morris Soublet, Sr., John Gilbert, and James Barnes were ordained deacons in the diocese's first deacon class.

Local African Americans played an important role on the national stage as well. In 1973, Guillory served as president of the National Black Catholic Caucus. Father Matthews served on the board of the National Black Seminarians Association and later the National Catholic Conference on Interracial Justice. Sister Toinette Eugene served as associate director of the National Black Sisters' Conference.

In 1973, Father Howard was appointed vicar for African American Catholics. In 1978, he was succeeded by Father Hillary Cooper, who was succeeded by Father Jay Matthews in 1983. In 1988, the Black Catholic Vicariate became known as the Black Catholic Pastoral Center and placed under the direction of Sister Marie de Porres Taylor, who had long been active in the vicariate.

In the early 1980s, a series of Black Catholic revivals were offered to "provide a wider experience of the Black religious experience." The revivals were planned in conjunction with the Allen Temple Baptist Church—the first three nights were held at Allen Temple and the last three at the Cathedral concluding with a major liturgy. Traditional forms of black spirituality, preaching, and singing were showcased. The revivals continued into the 1990s.

In 1986, the first Diocesan Black Catholic Congress was held at Sacred Heart parish with Sister Thea Bowman providing the keynote address. The Congress was held to "explore the concerns of Black Catholics," and to "affirm and recognize the gifts of Black Catholics."

As of 2001, the African American Catholic Pastoral Center, under the direction of Dr. Toinette Eugene, continues to oversee African American Catholic affairs in the diocese. The Center continues to foster an authentic African American Catholic spirituality and attempts to involve African Americans in the decision making process of the local Church.

Asians

Since the increase of Asian immigration in the early 1980s, Asians immigrants have played an increasingly important role in the diocese. Bishop Cummins has shown especial solicitude toward this group. In 1982, he became the U.S. delegate to the Federation of Asian Bishops Conferences, a role he continued until 2000. In 1997, at the Synod of America, Cummins made an important intervention on the need for a "pastoral response" to the increased Asian presence in the United States. Bishop Cummins was also selected to represent the American Bishops at the Asian Synod in Rome.

Filipinos

The largest Asian Catholic group are the Filipinos. The first wave of Filipino immigrants began arriving during the 1920s, though this diminished during the Depression of the 1930s. Immigration escalated once more following World War II. Most Filipino immigrants in this era obtained low-paying jobs in agriculture, industry or domestic service. The largest wave of Filipino immigrants began to arrive after 1965; by 1970, more than 13,000 Filipinos were living in Alameda and Contra Costa counties. By 2000, Filipinos made up more than 15 percent of the Catholic community in the diocese, totaling more than 100,000. The post-1965 immigration included a majority of professional and college educated immigrants, enabling this wave to establish themselves firmly in the middle class. The largest concentrations of Filipino settlement have been in West Contra Costa County and the Hayward-Fremont area. Parishes with the largest Filipino congregants are St. Joseph in Pinole, St. Anne in Union City, Our Lady of Good Counsel and St. Leander's in San Leandro, St. Paul in San Pablo, St. Patrick's in Rodeo, St. Barnabas in Alameda, Our Lady, Queen of the World, Pittsburg, and Holy Spirit in Fremont. Mass in Tagalog was first offered at St. Mary's Parish in Oakland in 1971, and currently three parishes offer such Masses, though most Filipinos attend English-speaking parishes.

As was the case with other groups, a vicariate for the Filipinos was set up in 1974 with Father Breccio P. Omega appointed first vicar, and traditional celebrations and devotions encouraged. Traditional celebrations include *Simbang Gabi*, a traditional novena of Masses held in preparation for Christmas, celebrated at dawn; *Salubong*, the encounter of the risen Christ with His sorrowing mother, celebrated at dawn on Easter morning; *Flores de Mayo*, devotion to Mary similar to the traditional May crowning; *Hesus Nazareno*, devotion to the suffering Jesus carrying the cross, and the *Santo Nino*, honoring the infant Jesus. Many parishes have begun celebrating these events. Filipinos also have an intense devotion to the rosary, and Marian celebrations, such as the devotion to Our Lady of Perpetual Help, are also popular.

In 1979, Father Ives Aniban replaced Father Omega, and in 1982, he was joined by Stanley Lee, who became a permanent deacon in 1988. At about that time the Filipino Pastoral Center was created under the direction of Deacon Lee. The main task of the Center was to help the new

Salubong at St. Barnabas, 1994

immigrant adjust, and to provide a sense of welcome. The Center hoped to involve Filipinos more deeply in their local parish communities. The Center created a New Immigrant Committee to attend directly to this problem.

As with the other pastoral centers, the Filipino pastoral center seeks to preserve the faith of the immigrant in a new setting. Particularly important in this regard have been the Filipino Catholic Organization, founded in 1950, and the Filipino Cursillo, first offered in 1972. Both have assisted the development of lay leaders, and have encouraged the traditional celebrations. The growing Filipino population ensures that Filipino Catholics will play an ever increasing role in diocesan affairs.

The Vietnamese

Few Vietnamese resided in the Bay Area prior to and during the Vietnam War. After the fall of Saigon in 1975, however, thousands of refugees fled Vietnam to escape the Communist regime. Though Catholics represented less than ten percent of the general population in Vietnam, the number of Catholics among the refugees was estimated at close to 40 percent. Many Catholics were dual refugees—they had first fled from North Vietnam after the Communist takeover there in 1954. Many Oakland Catholic families, acting through Diocesan Catholic Charities,

sponsored refugee families. In 1975, eleven parishes adopted families. By the end of 1975, more than 700 refugees had been resettled by Catholic Charities. Overseeing the resettlement was Vietnamese Sister Elisabeth Lang, who became director of the Catholic Charities Indochinese Resettlement Program.

The Vietnamese community grew with two additional waves of immigrants. A second wave of Vietnamese refugees crested around 1980, with the "boat people," refugees who fled their country by sea using any available means, and a third wave of Vietnamese arrived after 1986 as part of the Orderly Departure Program. The majority of immigrants settled in the San Jose area, where a personal parish for Vietnamese was established in 1999. By 1996, however, close to 17,000 Vietnamese were present in the Oakland Diocese, of which about 4,000 were Catholic.

The first Vietnamese Mass was celebrated on October 27, 1975 at St. Leo's in Oakland by

Vietnamese Sisters profession, 2001 (Luis Gris photo)

Vietnamese Marian procession

Father Tran Dinh Phuc, CSSR, with about 150 people attending. Over the next twenty-five years the community grew dramatically so that by 2001, Masses in Vietnamese were being offered in seven parishes—St. Anthony, St. Mary-St. Francis de Sales, and St. Lawrence O'Toole in Oakland, St. Felicitas in San Leandro, Our Lady Queen of the World in Bay Point, St. Paul in San Pablo, and Queen of All Saints in Concord. In 1983, Father Tran Thuc Dinh was appointed vicar for the Vietnamese. And in 1993, Father Dominic Nguyen Hoai Thuong was appointed Director of the Vietnamese Center.

Particularly important to the Vietnamese community in the diocese has been the work of the Quinhon Missionary Sisters of the Holy Cross also known as the Lovers of the Holy Cross. The order was established in the diocese by Sister Rosaline Nguyen, who presently serves as the Director of the Vietnamese Pastoral Center for the Diocese. In addition, the Order established a novitiate at St. Agnes parish in Concord and a Postulant House at Santa Maria parish in Orinda.

The Chinese

Though the number of Chinese in the Bay Area is quite large, the number of Chinese Catholics is small—about one percent of all Chinese. Nonetheless, in 1969, Father Matthias Lu, professor of logic and philosophy at St. Mary's and Holy Names Colleges, was appointed diocesan vicar for the Chinese. Mass in Mandarin was offered at Holy Spirit Newman Hall. In 1973, the first Pastoral Council of Chinese was held at Holy Spirit in Newman to assess the community's needs.

In 1984, Father Thomas Ng, a native of Hong Kong, was appointed Vicar for the Cantonese-speaking Chinese. Mass began being offered at St. Leo's in Oakland, and here the largest Chinese congregation began to develop. In 1987, a Chinese Pastoral Center was opened at 1322 Webster Street in Oakland's Chinatown to provide a Chinese Catholic presence there. A major celebration for the Chinese is the annual Chinese New Year's Mass at which the Blessing of the Ancestors is celebrated.

A novel undertaking by the diocese was the support and creation of a Friendship House—IFHA—at the University of California at Berkeley in 1999 by Father Bernard Chu, SJ.. The House provides welcome and accommodation for Chinese scholars studying in Berkeley.

Presently the Chinese pastoral center provides for the celebration of the liturgy in both Mandarin and Cantonese. Strong communities exist at St. Leo's; Holy Rosary in Union City, and St. Joseph's in Fremont. Occasionally a Mass in Mandarin is celebrated at St. John's in El Cerrito.

The Koreans

The Korean Catholic Community is of recent origin. As of 1965, there were only about 5,000 Koreans in the Bay Area, few of whom were Catholic. By 1985, the Catholic community in the diocese had grown to the point that a Korean Mass was offered by Father Kim Dong Whan at St. Leander's in San Leandro. The first Korean Catholic Council, under the presidency of Mr. Jong Kyu Yi, was instrumental in establishing the St. Andrew Kim Pastoral Center at the old

Archbishop Dominic Tang concelebrates Mass with Father Matthias Lu, to his right; Icon of Our Lady of China before the altar

St. Anne's Church in Union City with Father Lawrence Kim, OSB, obtained as chaplain. The community consisted of about 100 families. By 1999, the Center had moved to St. Cyril in Oakland under the leadership of Father Paul Oh, and the community had grown close to 2,000.

The Kmhmu'

The Kmhmu' are refugees from war-torn Laos, who fled their country in the mid-1970s following the Communist takeover. By 1985, about two hundred families, about half of whom were Catholics, had gathered under the clan leadership of a young man, Kan Souriya. Working with Father Peter Phavasiri, OMI, pastoral services were begun for the small community at St. Mark's parish in Richmond. The Kmhmu' Pastoral Center took form. Three Filipina women, Lui Gonzales, Angela Nagrampa and Mila Herrera, began the catechetical instruction for the children, youth, and adults. In 1991, Father Don MacKinnon, CSSR, and Sister Michaela O'Connor SHF, continued the ministry to the Khmhu'. Presently the weekly Mass is celebrated at St. Paul's in San Pablo. The community now operates a Kmhmu' center located in Richmond, where all pastoral services are provided. The community now numbers 125 families.

Kmhmu' celebrate 10th year of ministry of Father Don MacKinnon, CSSR, and Sister Michaela O'Connor, SHF (Photo Courtesy of Charlotte Hall)

The Polish

Few Polish Catholics lived in the Bay Area prior to 1980. Then with the social disruptions generated by the Solidarity Movement in Poland, a significant influx to the Bay Area began. By the mid-1990s there were more than 12,000 in the diocese. In the early 1980s, many of the Polish gathered around Father Leon Degner at St. Anne's in Walnut Creek. Degner had fled Poland following World War II. With Degner's death in 1985, a Polish Pastoral Center was established with Polish-born Father Leszak Bartoszewski at the helm. In 1987, the East Bay Polish-American Association constructed a building in Martinez, which included a chapel named Our Lady, Mother of Immigrants, that came to be used by the pastoral center. In 1991, the Pope John Paul II Polish Language School was opened at St. Catherine's in Martinez to insure that the Polish language and culture would be passed to the next generation. In 1993, the Polish Pastoral Center moved to Union City to join with the Korean and Deaf Pastoral centers in using the old St. Anne's Church. Out of this emerged the Holy Family Catholic Ethnic Mission.

Other Groups

The Diocese consists of far more ethnic groups than mentioned above. Large numbers of Portuguese continued to arrive in the 1970s, so several Portuguese Pastoral Centers were opened. In recent years, Portuguese immigration has significantly diminished, but the Brazilian community is on the rise. Many other groups established pastoral centers or communities as well, including the Asian-Indian, Sri Lankan, Pakistani, Ge'ez, Haitian, Indonesian, and Tongan. All of the centers are designed to give welcome to the immigrant. As Sister Felicia Sarati put it, "They need a place of welcome and a place where they can feel at home with their expression of faith." And what Father Bartoszewski concluded of the Polish Center could also apply to many others as well: "It's the center not only of religious activities, but also of cultural and social life. Our pastoral center helps in solving family problems, legal questions, even in finding a job."

The Deaf

The diocese has a long tradition of service to the deaf and hard of hearing community. In 1894, Mrs. Margaret McCourtney gave her house at the corner of 40th Street and Telegraph in Oakland to the Sisters of St. Joseph of Carondelet to open a school for the deaf. According to Carrie McClish, who wrote its history, St. Joseph's Home, as it was first called, opened on May 13, 1895, "the only Catholic institution of its kind on the Pacific Coast." The school and sisters did remarkable work until 1939, when the building was deemed a fire hazard and the school closed. Despite the school's closing, Monsignor William F. Reilly, director of Deaf Work from 1933 to 1958, kept several sisters at work in the religious education of deaf children. In 1951, he succeeded in opening St. Joseph's Center for the Deaf, "the first Catholic Center for the deaf in the United States." Mass was offered twice on Sunday for the deaf community. Reilly was succeeded by Monsignor Michael D. O'Brien who served the deaf community until 1983. The School for the Deaf was re-opened in 1963 at St. Francis de Sales. After several moves and a dwindling enrollment, the school finally closed in 1983. The Center remained open, however, operating out of Sacred Heart parish in Oakland. In December 1992, the Center moved to the old church at St. Anne's parish in Union City, and became part of the Holy Family Catholic Ethnic Center with the Koreans and Polish. Ardith

Lynch, Director of the Center since 1987, was named co-administrator of the new parish. The deaf community continues to celebrate "signed' Masses at the new center and at Sacred Heart.

Our Lady, Mother of Immigrants Chapel in Martinez; Icon of Our Lady of Czestochowa

Old St. Anne's, now Holy Family Catholic Ethnic Mission, used by Koreans, Polish, and the Deaf community

CHAPTER

9

JUBILEE 2000 AND BEYOND

The Diocese responded positively, stopping to reflect on the Jubilee themes of justice and reconciliation. Five pilgrimage sites were established: Mission San Jose, St. Elizabeth Seton in Pleasanton, Our Lady Queen of the World in Bay Point, St. Mary-St. Francis de Sales in Oakland, and St. Paul in San Pablo, and pilgrims were encouraged to reflect on the Jubilee themes as well.

Pope John Paul II declared the year 2000 a year of Jubilee in preparation for the new millennium.

victims of clerical sexual abuse to come forward. "Our first concern is to offer immediate and appropriate care to the victims and their families." With the assistance of Light, Flannery began holding small, breakfast gatherings of survivors, listening to their stories. In 1999, as the jubilee theme of reconciliation was being considered, it seemed natural to Flannery and Danielson for the Diocese to offer an apology to victims of clergy abuse.

The Diocese Apologizes

The diocese took the Pope's call to examine historic transgressions seriously. A committee

Bishop Cummins at Clergy Abuse Apology Ceremony (Chris Duffey photo)

On March 25, 2000, in what *The Voice* called "a move unprecedented in the

headed by Father Dan Danielson reflected on a number of past sins, but the issue that was most forthrightly addressed was the issue of clergy sexual abuse. As early as 1993, Terrie Hall Light of Hayward had formed the West Coast chapter of a support group called SNAP—Survivors Network of those Abused by Priests—and had asked the diocese to apologize for past abuse. The project picked up steam in 1995 through the efforts of newly appointed Chancellor Sister Barbara Flannery. Flannery publicly asked for all

history of the Church in Oakland," (and in the US Church for that matter), Bishop Cummins, speaking on behalf of the diocese, offered an apology to the victims of clerical abuse at a "reconciliation and healing" service held at Leona Lodge in Oakland. "The Jubilee call of the Holy Father encourages us to be reconciled with all whom Church people may have harmed or sinned against. The Diocese of Oakland, in solidarity with the Universal Church, expresses our remorse for past behavior toward the abused, acknowledges the Church's wrongdoing and seeks the forgiveness of those who have been sexually abused by the Church's clerical leaders and those who have not found a compassionate and pastoral response to such abuse whenever it occurred." More than 130 people attended, and as *The Voice* recorded, "pain, anger, and healing surged through Leona Lodge." Several personal testimonies evoked many tears, but Terrie Light observed, "The process itself of putting this service together has been so healing."

The Pilgrim Image of Our Lady of Guadalupe

The diocese sponsored two other major events during the Jubilee year, both of which celebrated the diocese's multicultural make up. Or as Father Stephan Kappler, event chair, put it, "All who have come to America have brought their richness and their gifts to make us who we are." On Saturday, October 28, the diocese held a Jubilee Pilgrimage honoring the Pilgrim Image of Our Lady of Guadalupe. The Image, a replica of the original, had been blessed by Pope John Paul II in Mexico City in 1999, and had begun a pilgrimage through the Americas. On October

Terrie Hall Light, director of SNAP, at Apology Ceremony (Chris Duffey photo)

27, the image arrived at Oakland's Jack London Square via boat from San Francisco, greeted by a festive, though prayerful, gathering of the faithful. The following day the Jubilee Pilgrimage was celebrated at Oakland's Kaiser Convention Center. Despite a steady downpour of rain, more than 4,000 pilgrims appeared and their spirits could not be dampened as they processed through the streets of Oakland. Inside the convention center, the Image was greeted by an Aztec dance group, followed by children carrying flags of many nations. Next, groups representing

Pilgrim Image brought to Oakland (Arturo Vera photo)

The Pilgrim Image of Our Lady of Guadalupe arrives at Jack London Square (Arturo Vera photo)

CHAPTER 9

Seminarians present Pilgrim image to crowd at Kaiser Convention Center, Oakland (Chris Duffey photo)

Rain did not deter a joyous procession through the streets (Chris Duffey photo)

each of the five major continents appeared in native dress. Ethnic choirs completed the aura which reflected the deep cultural richness of the diocese. A parade of floats and banners brought the day to an end. The gathering was addressed by Bishop Cummins; by Cardinal Juan Sandoval, Archbishop of Guadalajara; and Jerry Brown, Mayor of Oakland.

For the next two weeks the Image travelled from parish to parish, where prayer and veneration services were hosted.

Jubilee Mass

On November 11, 2000 the Jubilee year reached its climax with a Eucharistic liturgy held at the Oakland Coliseum Arena, planned by a committee headed by Father Mark Wiesner. More than 18,000 came to celebrate, the largest single gathering in the history of the diocese. Participants were treated to spectacular performances prior to the Mass as the various ethnic choirs performed. The Pilgrim Image was brought on to the floor for its final appearance in the diocese. The old bell from St. Francis de Sales was rung. The liturgy itself reflected the multicultural quality of the diocese, and Bishop Cummins spoke of the diocese as a "Galillee of Nations." Prayers and readings were offered in English, Spanish, Tagalog, Vietnamese, Korean, Polish, Portuguese, and Chinese. The Arena exploded at the recessional hymn, singing Jesse Manibusan's "Malo! Malo! Thanks be to God!" in which God is thanked in thirteen different languages in a call and response with the leader Jesse Manibusan. All left the Arena with a feeling of renewal and a determination to live out Bishop Cummins' call to them to be "a leaven to the world."

Jubilee Mass at Oakland Coliseum Arena, November 11, 2000 (Chris Duffey photo)

*Banners decorated the Kaiser Convention Center
(Chris Duffey photo)*

Gifts presented at the Offertory (Luis Gris photo)

A HISTORY OF THE DIOCESE OF
OAKLAND

*Deacons proclaim the Gospel
(Chris Duffey photo)*

Multicultural Choir (Luis Gris photo)

A New Cathedral

Since 1989, the year of the Loma Prieta earthquake, the diocese had been without a cathedral. Various churches throughout the diocese had hosted major diocesan events, but in 2000, Bishop Cummins decided it was time to move ahead with a new Cathedral. Brother Mel Anderson, FSC, former president of St. Mary's College, was appointed to staff a committee commissioned to explore the possibility of a new cathedral. Brother Mel stressed the importance of a new cathedral. "A cathedral is the Mother Church...It is a sign of unity, a central gathering place in times of joyous celebrations as well as in moments of crisis. It is a sign of moral stability, unity and hope, in a skeptical, contentious and diverse society." The committee made a bold choice in selecting renowned architect Dr. Santiago Calatrava as the design architect. Dr. Calatrava produced an extraordinary model of the new Cathedral appropriately to be called "The Cathedral of Christ the Light." The design "will flood the interior with light." The structure takes as its source the Vatican II document *Lumen gentium*, Christ, the light to all peoples. Billed as "A Cathedral for the Third Millennium," its

theme is in keeping with the historic resolve of the diocese—to implement the teachings of the Second Vatican Council. It is fitting that a diocese which has prided itself on being a Vatican II diocese, will now have a cathedral that reflects this reality in concept, design, and symbol.

As this book goes to press, the cathedral is still in the planning stage and still faces many battles. A site on Lake Merritt is under consideration, but protests have already arisen. Fundraising remains a concern, as Bishop Cummins has promised that money would not be taken from any current programs. Despite all the difficulties, the vision and foresight provided so far, ensure that the project will come to a happy conclusion. As the Cathedral Mission statement concludes, "As the Church enters the new millennium, and as the City of Oakland renews itself, a cathedral in the heart of the city will be a center of faith, celebration, music, and the arts for our diocese. It will be a place of solace and of outreach serving the compelling needs of our society, welcoming and lifting the spirits of all people."

A Cathedral for the Third Millennium

Cathedral brochure

Interior of proposed Cathedral of Light

CONCLUSION

As the Diocese of Oakland enters the third millennium and the fifth decade of its history, it does so with many blessings. Its blessings include its great diversity of peoples; it includes the vast number of the People of God, who dedicate their services and gifts to the building of the Kingdom of God in Oakland. We are a richly blessed church, and in the words of Jesse Manibusan we sing, "Malo! Malo! Thanks be to God!"

But for all our riches the Gospel challenge remains—to bring the Good News to a world "desperately in need of good news"; to be a sign of hope in a world desperately crying out for hope. In short, to be a witness to the Risen Christ, so that His Presence may become known. This is our task. This is our commitment. We are the Church!

A Parish *Family Album*

ST. CORNELIUS, RICHMOND (1952)

St. Cornelius Parish is celebrating its Golden Jubilee. It was established in 1952. The parish school was founded in 1949 by the Sisters of Notre Dame, Cleveland. The parish has a heavy concentration of Spanish-speaking families.

ST. DAVID OF WALES, RICHMOND (1952)

The first Mass of the new parish of St. David was offered at the Slav Hall on Palm Sunday, April 6, 1952. Fifty years later, St. David's has a full compliment of parish buildings, including a school founded in 1963, conducted by the Sisters of Notre Dame of Cleveland. Recent restoration work includes installation of the original stained glass windows and plans to restore the original altar. Many of the original "founding fathers and mothers" are still active parishioners.

ST. FELICITAS, SAN LEANDRO (1952)

Founded in February of 1952, St Felicitas Church has become a very active multicultural parish 50 years later. The first church, which now serves as the parish social hall and gymnasium was dedicated in March 1953. St Felicitas School was opened February 1959, by the Sisters of St Joseph of Wichita. Because of the constant growth of families in the parish the "new" church was built and dedicated in May, 1968. The parish celebrates weekly liturgies in English, Spanish and Vietnamese and is served by a staff of priests, Sisters and lay persons. At the heart of the parish life is the Eucharist which serves as the strength and inspiration for the ministries that complete the parish life.

ST. CALLISTUS, EL SOBRANTE (1952)

In 1952, Father Michael Ryan became the first pastor of St. Callistus, which was made up predominantly of Irish and Italian families. He oversaw the building of the first church. His quiet manner and holiness are still remembered today by elderly parishioners.

During the 1980s, a significant population of Filipinos began arriving in the parish. Devotions to Our Mother of Perpetual Help grew at this time. In the 1990s, the first parish council was established. The Sisters of the Holy Family were in charge of the religious education of youth until 1995. The parish looks forward to the challenges of growth and expansion as it celebrates its Golden Jubilee.

ST. FRANCIS OF ASSISI, CONCORD (1955)

Most Precious Blood Parish, the name was changed to St. Francis of Assisi in 1984, was founded in 1955 to serve the growing Concord area. The first church was dedicated in October 1956. The founding pastor, Monsignor Edward Varni, served as pastor until 1991. In 1965 the Sisters of St. Joseph of Carondelet opened the parish school. In 1983 a tragic arson fire destroyed the church and the worshiping community moved to the multi-purpose building until the new church was built. The new St. Francis of Assisi Church was dedicated in 1985. The spectacular mosaic tile scenes of the Crucifixion of Christ, Stations of the Cross and biblical events were created by Gesa St. Galy for the old church. Some of the tiles were salvaged by parishioners, who hand sorted through the ashes and debris. Many pieces were reused in the new church.

The parish serves a widely diverse, ethnically mixed community well represented in lay leadership.

Mosaic tile scene of crucifixion by artist Gesa St. Galy saved from 1983 fire by parishioners

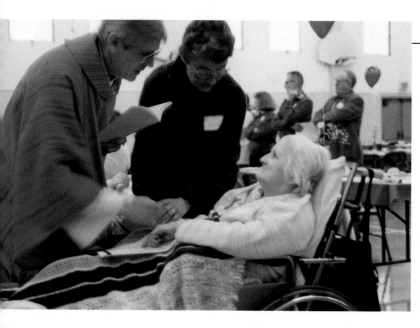

ST. BEDE, HAYWARD (1955)

The Archdiocese of San Francisco established the Parish of St. Bede in 1955. It has become a multi-ethnic community. This is reflected, particularly, in the devotional life and many diverse devotional practices of the community. Multicultural/religious celebrations and fiestas have become normative in the life of the parish. The Eucharist is the heart and unifying principle of all these celebrations. From this has flowed an ever-expanding outreach program striving to meet the diverse needs of the community and also that of the larger civic community. The collaborative leadership of the clergy, staff of the parish and the Parish Council has made this possible.

Father Seamus Farrell at the annual Parish Mass and anointing of homebound, residents from convalescent hospitals followed by special lunch

A Parish *Family Album*

ST. PASCHAL BAYLON, OAKLAND (1955)

Situated in the Oakland Hills, the parish was established in 1955. The parish emphasized Catholic education, beginning its school before it constructed the church. Today, the parish is known for its innovative liturgical music.

ST. ALPHONSUS LIGUORI, SAN LEANDRO (1955)

Established in 1955, the parish was placed under the care of the Congregation of the Most Holy Redeemer. The Redemptorists ably served the parish until 1983. In 1998, Deacon George Peters was appointed administrator.

ST. BONAVENTURE, CONCORD (1957)

St. Bonaventure was established in 1957 to serve the growing population of the Clayton Valley. The "school building" was used as a church until 1985 when it became the social hall. The new church was designed with lots of glass to include the wonderful outdoor scenery and wood paneling for interior warmth. St. Bonaventure is known for its hospitality and Christian outreach. The long awaited school is currently on the planning boards.

TRANSGURATION, CASTRO VALLEY (1961)

In April of 1961, Transfiguration came into being, the second parish in Castro Valley. Our beginnings were very humble; the first Mass was celebrated in a garage, then moved into a grape arbor. Finally, just before the rains came, we moved indoors to a dog kennel, nicknamed "St. Bernard's," along with fleas. Construction began in 1962 and by 1980 the parish plant included a new church. This parish has been blessed with caring, energetic pastors and dedicated deacons.

This friendly, family-oriented parish looks forward to meeting the needs and challenges that the new millennium will bring to the community and the parish.

Outdoor Mass at Transfiguration, Castro Valley

ST. RAYMOND PEÑAFORT, DUBLIN (1961)

Although not an established parish, by 1860 St. Raymond's had its community and church. Four acres had been donated by two men who had crossed the Sierra two years before the Donner Party tragedy. The new St. Raymond of Peñafort Parish plant has little resemblance to the 1860 church. The early experience of community, however, continues to this day.

Father John Murphy (1961-1970), the first pastor, labored in primitive conditions to bring the newly established parish into being. He died in an automobile accident in 1970. Monsignor Bernard Moran was appointed in February 1970 and quickly began to enlarge the parish plant and instituted Stewardship. A school was added to the plant in 1986. The beautiful modern church is the center of the community.

OUR LADY QUEEN OF THE WORLD, BAY POINT (1962)

In 1962 Our Lady, Queen of the World was chosen as the patron of the newly established Diocese of Oakland and the name of the first parish established by Bishop Floyd Begin. It serves the area of West Pittsburg in what is today Bay Point. Two mission churches, St. Frances of Rome in Port Chicago and St. Philomena in Bella Vista, served the area before the current parish. The church and rectory were built by volunteers and stand today as a reminder of the spirit and progress made by the Church in Contra Costa County. Many parish organizations serve this growing community.

New main sign installed by volunteers, March 2001

First wedding in new chapel, June 16, 2001

ST. AGNES, CONCORD (1964)

St. Agnes parish was founded in 1964 in order to serve the rapidly growing Concord area. Various facilities have been used over the past thirty-six years, including the Elk's Hall. Construction for the existing church was begun in December, 1981, and the building dedicated in September, 1983. Plans for a new Ministry Center/Office Building are progressing towards completion. St. Agnes has evolved into a true Stewardship Parish, serving the central Concord area with its large Filipino-American and Hispanic communities through eighty-four separate ministries.

Gathering of parishioners following Mass; brown cross symbol of parish

ST. CHARLES BORROMEO, LIVERMORE (1964)

The community of St. Charles Borromeo, established in 1964, prides itself in being "not a place where, but a people who". The small, 800-family parish supports over 40 different ministry groups. They recently built the multipurpose Keeley Center which provides the parish with a place to meet, teach and better serve the community. Father Richard McCafferty, SJ, is the current Administrator.

GOOD SHEPHERD, PITTSBURG (1965)

Good Shepherd Parish in Pittsburg was established in 1965. It is an ethnically mixed parish, about 60% Filipino, with a significant community of Latinos as well.

ST. ANDREW-ST. JOSEPH, OAKLAND (1965)

St. Joseph was the first Portuguese parish in 1892 and St. Andrew started in 1907 after the earthquake to host refugees. St. Andrew and St. Joseph parishes, which merged in 1965, has a long history of leadership. It is an ethnically mixed parish. Predominantly African American and Latino, parishioners jointly serve the poor, hungry, sick and elderly through the weekday Soup kitchen, Oakland Community Organization, many other active organizations, classes and festive events. Three permanent deacons have served the parish continuously for decades. In October 2000, Holy Names Sister Marian Wright was installed by Bishop Cummins as this parish's first Parish Life Director to serve the parishioners daily needs.

Church celebration, 2000

ST. ANNE, WALNUT CREEK (1965)

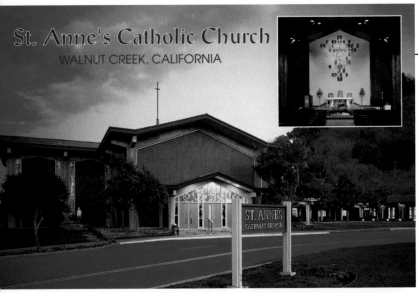

The parish of St. Anne is dedicated to serve a particular area of Walnut Creek which includes Rossmoor Retirement Community. Approximately 91% of parish families are residents of Rossmoor.

Our parish Mission Statement says: The mission of our parish is to help each other experience Christ as the center of our lives and to know that we are destined for eternal life with our God. The special emphasis of our mission is Stewardship as a Way of Life. It is a newfound emphasis on sharing our time, talent and treasure in gratitude to God who has given us all that we are and all that we have.

ST. JOHN VIANNEY, WALNUT CREEK (1965)

Founded in 1965, the parish, from its inception, has witnessed a very active laity in keeping with the mandate of the Second Vatican Council.

A Parish *Family Album*

Pancake breakfast

Father Thomas Duong Binh-Minh (pastor, 1998-2001) with shrine to Our Lady of Penafrancia

ST. MONICA, MORAGA (1965)

Nineteen-sixty-five was a very good year, a vintage year for California wine, and May 4, 1965 a red-letter day for the City of Moraga. On that date, on the feast of St. Monica, a parish bearing her name was established. From a pear orchard arose a mighty parish plant that includes a beautiful church and an active, caring community that reaches out to those in need. For a number of years, prior to the building of the church, Mass was celebrated at the Chapel of St. Mary's College. Bishop Floyd Begin dedicated the parish church on October 5, 1975.

This is one of the busiest parishes in the diocese with full and active participation of the laity. Cath McGhee, the present Parochial Administrator, was the first lay administrator in the Diocese of Oakland and under her leadership the parish continues to flourish.

OUR LADY OF GOOD COUNSEL, SAN LEANDRO (1966)

Our Lady of Good Counsel Parish began life as Star of the Sea mission of St. Felicitas Parish in order to better serve the 350 Catholic families of the Mulford Garden area of San Leandro. On July 1, 1966, Bishop Floyd Begin established a parish in that area and named it Our Lady of Good Counsel. The Blue Dolphin Restaurant at the San Leandro Marina served as worship space on Sundays until the current church was completed in 1969.

The parishioners of Our Lady of Good Counsel are rich in cultural diversity, and are actively involved in all parish ministries as well as a communal seat of Marian devotions.

ST. STEPHEN, WALNUT CREEK (1966)

Bishop Floyd Begin established St. Stephen Parish in 1966 from portions of two larger neighboring parishes. Although small in size, the St. Stephen community enjoys an active and vibrant faith with a high level of lay involvement in parish ministries and outreach programs. Our founding pastor, Monsignor Joseph Keaveny, instilled in parishioners from the very beginning this spirit of cooperation and collaboration that continue to make St. Stephen Parish what it is today. The church building, the first in the Oakland Diocese designed by the well-known architect Aaron Green, was completed in 1971. It is nestled amidst the pastoral background of the Acalanes Ridge Open Space and will soon share its bucolic site with the new Father Harry B. Morrison Parish Center, scheduled for completion in December, 2001.

Bishop Cummins celebrates Mass at the groundbreaking ceremony for the new parish hall, April, 2001.

HOLY SPIRIT/NEWMAN HALL, BERKELEY (1967)

Newman Hall and the Paulist Fathers have been serving the Catholic students of the University of California since 1899. In 1967 it became – in addition – Holy Spirit Parish serving the south side of Berkeley. The youth and intellectual challenge of the university invigorates the parish life; and the experience of family life, age and childhood, as well as diverse careers, expands the boundaries of academia.

ST. JAMES THE APOSTLE, FREMONT (1972):

On April 13, 1972 Bishop Begin created the Parish of St. James the Apostle in Fremont. Although remaining small, St. James offers a very friendly environment where parishioners know one another, socialize and offer support when difficult times arise. The parish shows concern for other communities, including St. Mary's, a Navajo Mission in New Mexico. St. Vincent de Paul Society is very active in St. James the Apostle Parish.

ST. ANNE, UNION CITY (1973)

Though not established as a parish until 1973, St. Anne's has served as a mission since 1860. It has served a succession of immigrant communities—Portuguese (1880s), Mexicans (1950s), and Filipinos (1970s-). A church was built and dedicated in 1926—it currently houses the Holy Family Catholic Ethnic Mission. A new church was built and dedicated in 1983. The first pastor was Father Eladio Pascual. The parish continues its historic ministry of caring for the faith of an immigrant population.

A Parish
Family Album

ST. ALBERT THE GREAT, ALAMEDA (1976)

St. Albert, the first parish on Bay Farm Island, was established as the result of an endowment left by Mrs. Maude Marshall, a parishioner of St. Philip Neri. Her only requirement was that the parish be named St. Albert, in honor of her late husband. The first pastor was Father William Marshall (no relation to the benefactress!). The small parish has an active, dedicated laity and a beautiful spirit.

ST. JOAN OF ARC, SAN RAMON (1979)

ST. IGNATIUS OF ANTIOCH, ANTIOCH (1979)

St. Ignatius was founded on June 4, 1979. The first pastor was Father Robert Ponciroli. Until a parish center was built in 1987, Sunday Masses were conducted at Park Junior High School and Mission Elementary School. In 1997, under the leadership of Father Vincent Cotter, the Parish Center was remodeled to serve as the permanent worship space that it is today. An Angel Garden and Marian Grotto were erected next to the church. A parishioner created and donated the beautiful crucifix behind the altar. The parish community reflects a strong lay leadership and an active Filipino membership.

The vision for the future is to build a new church and renovate the existing building for a parish center. A new pastor, Father Geoffrey Baaran, was appointed in September 2001.

St. Joan of Arc Parish was established in 1979 out of the fast-growing communities of San Ramon and Danville. The parish began with worship in an elementary school library, moving into a newly built church in 1983. In 1991 a second ground-breaking was held to commence construction of a new parish center, containing offices, meeting space, classrooms and a gymnasium. The parish continues to boom and has exceeded 4,100 registered families. St. Joan of Arc grows ever stronger in its commitment to the religious strength of the community. Together we praise God, share our faith and care for those in need.

ST. ANNE, BYRON (1984)

In 1916 the Archbishop of San Francisco visited Byron and met with the local Catholic leaders to plan for a church in Byron. A 10 acre parcel of land was purchased for $10 in gold coin. The church was named "St. Anne, Mother of the Virgin Mary, Grandmother of Jesus", and dedicated in 1917. It was a mission of several parishes until 1984 when Father Robert Ponciroli was named pastor. The current pastor, Father Ron Schmit, was appointed in 1996. Sunday liturgy is celebrated at Discovery Bay school in order to accommodate the growing number of parishioners. In 2000 the registered families of St. Anne were nearly 600 and growing.

*Dedication of land
for new church,
July 2000*

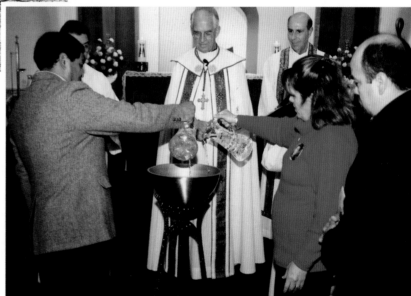

CONCORD
HISPANIC
COMMUNITY
(1989)
(see page 104)

HOLY FAMILY
CATHOLIC
ETHNIC MISSION
(1993)
(see page 111)

ST. LEONARD/ SANTA PAULA, FREMONT (2001)

St. Leonard-Santa Paula Parish was formed on January 1, 2001, when the two former parishes of St. Leonard and Santa Paula were merged. St. Leonard was established in 1959. Santa Paula was created from a portion of St. Leonard to become a parish in 1965. The newly merged parish serves an economically and ethically diverse community, with a large number of Spanish-speaking and Filipino Catholics.

The pastor of the combined parish is Father Larry Silva.

Installation of first pastor, Father Larry Silva. Parishioners representing two former parishes pour water into baptismal font. (Chris Duffey photo)

ACKNOWLEDGEMENTS

In completing a project of this type, many debts are incurred. I am grateful to all who have supported me in this work. Thanks to Bishop John S. Cummins, whose enthusiasm for history has made this a delightful project. Thanks to Sister Barbara Flannery, CSJ, for her always gracious support and facilitation. Thanks to Mary Carmen Batiza, who has dedicated her life to the service of the Church in Oakland and who was a joy to work with. Thanks to Dr. Judith Stanley, who conducted several oral history interviews, which greatly advanced the story. Thanks to Sister Felicia Sarati, CSJ, who provided helpful comments and beautiful photographs, as did Fathers Jay Matthews and William O'Donnell. Thanks to Monica Clark, who graciously provided access to the files of *The Catholic Voice*. Thanks to Father Don Osuna, for providing a copy of his unpublished memoir of his time at the Cathedral.

Thanks to the various archivists who provided photographs and information, especially Sister Michaela O'Connor of the Holy Family Sisters, Sister Madeleine Rita Murphy of the Sisters of the Holy Names, Sister Eileen Marie Egan of the Notre Dame Sisters, Sister Marilyn Gouailhardou of the Mercy Sisters, Sister Evangela Balde of the Mission San Jose Dominicans, Christine Catalano of the Presentation Sisters, and Brother Bertram Coleman of the Christian Brothers.

I would like to acknowledge especially the noted work of my predecessors, particularly Peter Conmy for his encyclopedic *History of the Diocese of Oakland*, and the extraordinary collection of oral history interviews put together by Don Wood as *An Oral History of Bishop Floyd Begin*. I would also like to acknowledge the profound influence the late Father Harry B. Morrison had on me—he was a superb, meticulous historian, who really should have been the one to write this text.

Finally, thanks to my wife, Sabina, who remained calm and supportive during some of the more trying times of this project.

Jeffrey M. Burns